EVERYMAN,
I WILL GO WITH THEE
AND BE THY GUIDE,
IN THY MOST
TO GO F

EVERYMAN'S LIBRARY
POCKET POETS

Christmas Poems

Selected and edited by
John Hollander and J. D. McClatchy

EVERYMAN'S LIBRARY

POCKET POETS

Alfred A. Knopf · New York · Toronto

THIS IS A BORZOI BOOK
PUBLISHED BY ALFRED A. KNOPF, INC.

This selection by John Hollander and J. D. McClatchy first published in
Everyman's Library, 1999

ISBN 0-375-40789-8

Library of Congress Cataloging-in-Publication Data
Christmas poems / selected and edited by John Hollander and
J. D. McClatchy.
p.   cm.—(Everyman's library pocket poets)
ISBN 0-375-40789-8 (alk. paper)
1. Christmas Poetry.   I. Hollander. John.   II. McClatchy, J. D.,
1945–   .   III. Series.
PN6110.C5C587   1999   99-36265
821.008′0334—dc21   CIP

Typography by Peter B. Willberg
Typeset in the UK by AccComputing, Castle Cary, Somerset
Printed and bound in Germany by
Graphischer Grossbetrieb Pössneck GmbH

CONTENTS

5

FOREWORD

Christmas is both a holiday and a holy day. At the end of the year and during its darkest days, a joyous festival of lights celebrates the world's redemption from death – whether by divine salvation or by the coming return of spring. At the center of this dramatic day is a child – or rather, a child and an old man. The child may be the infant Jesus or the allegorical figure of the new year, just as the old man is both Father Time with his scythe and hourglass and Father Christmas, St. Nicholas or Santa Claus with his sack of gifts. And from the start, the day has been associated with poetry, from the song of the seraphim above the manger to the cherished carols around the punchbowl. Like the heart itself, poetry is drawn instinctively to the marvelous. Like shepherd or king, the poets have come over the centuries to wonder and worship, to lay their gifts at the feet of a miraculous moment.

The day and year of Jesus's birth have always been uncertain. It wasn't until the fourth century AD that December 25th was settled on, and two centuries later it was declared the feast day. But of course, from the very beginning, and in every sun-worshiping culture, there had been festivals in late December and early January to celebrate at the winter solstice the return of light. Over time, the ceremonies grew more elaborate and ritualized, and paid tribute as well to the gods of plenty. In ancient Rome, for instance, the great week-long seasonal holiday was the Saturnalia, held in remembrance of the legendary Golden Age. As Christianity spread among the pagan peoples, festivals overlapped and merged, creating thereby a day that is observed both reverently and gaily.

For all the hushed grandiloquence of its rituals, Christmas is a domestic event, a cozy celebration of family and tradition. And it is largely a Victorian invention. Christmas trees were brought indoors first in Germany, and it is said that Martin Luther first decorated a tree with candles. The German Prince Albert, soon after his marriage to Queen Victoria, introduced the practice in England – which immigrants brought to America. But much earlier, of course, music and poetry had been at the heart of the celebration.

The poems gathered here trace the drama of both the feast and the celebration. From the Annunciation to the Epiphany, from 'twas-the-night-before anticipation to the untrimming of the tree, the poems catch up the wonder of Christmas. The grandest poems concentrate on the Nativity itself. Milton's magisterial ode, "On the Morning of Christs Nativity," sets the standard for sublimity, and poets from Donne to Yeats to Eliot have brooded on the miraculous birth as an event that transformed both history and the human heart. The mysteries of redemption and renewal have in turn prompted meditations on the meanings of Christmas that can be as visionary as Robert Southwell's "The Burning Babe," or as delicate as Anthony Hecht's "Illumination."

What collection of Christmas verse would be complete without Clement Moore's "A Visit from St. Nicholas," or without the carols whose words instinctively draw to mind their melodies from memories of Christmases past? But a day so bright as Christmas is bound also to make the shadows seem darker, and we have included poems by Thomas Hardy, Edwin Arlington Robinson, Mona Van Duyn and others that view the holiday and its celebration of innocence through the bitter lens of war and greed and homelessness.

And when the merry-makers have pushed back from the table, and the decorations have been put back in their boxes? As W. H. Auden has written, "To those who have seen / The Child, however dimly, however incredulously, / The Time Being is, in a sense, the most trying time of all." We return to our lives, and to the new year, as if from a dream. We resolve to learn again the lessons of love, to keep our word. Again, the poets capture that weary, wary moment – the moment just after "our tired earthliness" has been blessed.

No day in the year, no moment in our lives, is so steeped in memory and joy. We hope that the poems in this book – as if brightly boxed under the tree – will be shared as gifts with those you love.

ANNUNCIATION
AND ADVENT

THE ANNUNCIATION

Nothing will ease the pain to come
Though now she sits in ecstasy
And lets it have its way with her.
The angel's shadow in the room
Is lightly lifted as if he
Had never terrified her there.

The furniture again returns
To its old simple state. She can
Take comfort from the things she knows
Though in her heart new loving burns
Something she never gave to man
Or god before, and this god grows

Most like a man. She wonders how
To pray at all, what thanks to give
And whom to give them to. "Alone
To all men's eyes I now must go"
She thinks, "And by myself must live
With a strange child that is my own."

So from her ecstasy she moves
And turns to human things at last
(Announcing angels set aside).
It is a human child she loves
Though a god stirs beneath her breast
And great salvations grip her side.

ELIZABETH JENNINGS   17

ADVENT

Earth grown old, yet still so green,
    Deep beneath her crust of cold
Nurses fire unfelt, unseen:
    Earth grown old.

    We who live are quickly told:
Millions more lie hid between
    Inner swathings of her fold.

When will fire break up her screen?
    When will life burst thro' her mould?
Earth, earth, earth, thy cold is keen,
    Earth grown old.

ADVENT CALENDAR

Bethlehem in Germany,
Glitter on the sloping roofs,
Breadcrumbs on the windowsills,
Candles in the Christmas trees,
Hearths with pairs of empty shoes:
Panels of Nativity
Open paper scenes where doors
Open into other scenes,
Some recounted, some foretold.
Blizzard-sprinkled flakes of gold
Gleam from small interiors,
Picture-boxes in the stars
Open up like cupboard doors
In a cabinet Jesus built.

Southern German villagers,
Peasants in the mica frost,
See the comet streaming down,
Heavenly faces, each alone,
Faces lifted, startled, lost,
As if lightning lit the town.

Sitting in an upstairs window
Patiently the village scholar
Raises his nearsighted face,
Interrupted by the star.

Left and right his hands lie stricken
Useless on his heavy book.
When I lift the paper door
In the ceiling of his study
One canary-angel glimmers,
Flitting in the candelabra,
Peers and quizzes him: Rabbi,
What are the spheres surmounted by?
But his lips are motionless.
Child, what are you asking for?
Look, he gazes past the roofs,
Gazes where the bitter North,
Stretched across the empty place,
Opens door by door by door.

This is childhood's shrunken door.
When I touch the glittering crumbs,
When I cry to be admitted,
No one answers, no one comes.

And the tailor's needle flashes
In mid-air with thread pulled tight,
Stitching a baptismal gown.
But the gown, the seventh door,
Turns up an interior
Hidden from the tailor's eyes:
Baby presents like the boxes
Angels hold on streets and stairways,

Wooden soldier, wooden sword,
Chocolate coins in crinkled gold,
Hints of something bought and sold,
Hints of murder in the stars.

Baby's gown is sown with glitter
Spread across the tailor's lap.
Up above his painted ceiling
Baby mouse's skeleton
Crumbles in the mouse's trap.

Leaning from the cliff of heaven,
Indicating whom he weeps for,
Joseph lifts his lamp above
The infant like a candle-crown.
Let my fingers touch the silence
Where the infant's father cries.
Give me entrance to the village
From my childhood where the doorways
Open pictures in the skies.
But when all the doors are open,
No one sees that I've returned.
When I cry to be admitted,
No one answers, no one comes.
Clinging to my fingers only
Pain, like glitter bits adhering,
When I touch the shining crumbs.

CHRISTMAS EVE

CHRISTMAS EVE

Dark is the hour, long the night;
Hoarfrost sheds a shimmering light;
The wind in the naked woodland cries
A harplike music; the willow sighs.
But a marvellous quiet dwells in heaven –
Sirius, Markab, the faithful Seven –
For the Old Year's sands are well-nigh run;
This is the Birthday of the Sun.

No glint of dawn; but Chanticlere
Is crowing of Christmas, bugle clear.
In waxen hive, close-wintering,
Bees a slumbrous orison sing;
Roused from their lair in dales of the snow,
Light-foot deer in procession go;
Cattle and sheep in byre and pen
Kneel in the darkness, unseen of men:
For the Old Year's sands are well-nigh run;
This is the Birthday of the Sun.

Now houses of humans with jargonings ring,
Hautboy and serpent and flute and string,
Voices in gruff-shrill carolling –
Men and boys hunched up in the cold.
Tinkles the ice on the frozen mould.

Hesper is shining – rime on thatch;
Stag-borne Nicholas comes – unlatch!
Children stir in their dream and then
Drowsily sigh and turn over again.
Airs of the morn in the orchard flow;
Lo, in the apple boughs, mistletoe!
For the Old Year's sands are well-nigh run;
This is the Birthday of the Sun.

Master and Man, the East burns red;
Drowse no longer in sluggard bed;
Garland the Yule log; scatter the wheat –
Feast for the starving birds to eat.
Mistress and maid, wax warm you shall –
Boar in oven, burned wine, spiced ale,
There's quiring in heaven; and Gabriel
Wings from the zenith his news to tell;
Shepherd and king fare forth again –
Peace on earth, goodwill to men –
For, loving and lovely, in manger laid,
Dreams o'er her Babe the Virgin Maid.
Kindle then candles for your soul;
Shake off the net life's follies bring;
Ev'n of the innocent death takes toll;
There is an end to wandering.
But see, in cold clod the snowdrop blows;
Spring's inexhaustible fountain flows;

Love bides in earth till time is done;
The Old Year's sands are well-nigh run;
This is the Birthday of the Sun.

CHRISTMAS EVE

Christmas hath a darkness
   Brighter than the blazing noon,
Christmas hath a chillness
   Warmer than the heat of June,
Christmas hath a beauty
   Lovelier than the world can show:
For Christmas bringeth Jesus,
   Brought for us so low.

Earth, strike up your music,
   Birds that sing and bells that ring;
Heaven hath answering music
   For all Angels soon to sing:
Earth, put on your whitest
   Bridal robe of spotless snow:
For Christmas bringeth Jesus,
Brought for us so low.

From IN MEMORIAM

CIV

The time draws near the birth of Christ;
    The moon is hid, the night is still;
    A single church below the hill
Is pealing, folded in the mist.

A single peal of bells below,
    That wakens at this hour of rest
    A single murmur in the breast,
That these are not the bells I know.

Like strangers' voices here they sound,
    In lands where not a memory strays,
    Nor landmark breathes of other days,
But all is new unhallowed ground.

CV

Tonight ungathered let us leave
    This laurel, let this holly stand:
    We live within the stranger's land,
And strangely falls our Christmas-eve.

Our father's dust is left alone
    And silent under other snows:
    There in due time the woodbine blows,
The violet comes, but we are gone.

No more shall wayward grief abuse
    The genial hour with mask and mime;
    For change of place, like growth of time,
Has broke the bond of dying use.

Let cares that petty shadows cast,
    By which our lives are chiefly proved,
    A little spare the night I loved,
And hold it solemn to the past.

But let no footstep beat the floor,
    Nor bowl of wassail mantle warm;
    For who would keep an ancient form
Through which the spirit breathes no more?

Be neither song, nor game, nor feast;
    Nor harp be touched, nor flute be blown;
    No dance, no motion, save alone
What lightens in the lucid east.

Of rising worlds by yonder wood.
    Long sleeps the summer in the seed;
    Run out your measured arcs, and lead
The closing cycle rich in good.

NOEL: CHRISTMAS EVE, 1913

Pax hominibus benae voluntatis

A frosty Christmas Eve
   when the stars were shining
Fared I forth alone
   where westward falls the hill,
And from many a village
   in the water'd valley
Distant music reach'd me
   peals of bells aringing:
The constellated sounds
   ran sprinkling on earth's floor
As the dark vault above
   with stars was spangled o'er.

Then sped my thought to keep
   that first Christmas of all
When the shepherds watching
   by their folds ere the dawn
Heard music in the fields
   and marveling could not tell
Whether it were angels
   or the bright stars singing.

Now blessed be the tow'rs
   that crown England so fair

That stand up strong in prayer
    unto God for our souls:
Blessed be their founders
    (said I) an' our country folk
Who are ringing for Christ
    in the belfries to-night
With arms lifted to clutch
    the rattling ropes that race
Into the dark above
    and the mad romping din.

But to me heard afar
    it was starry music
Angels' song, comforting
    as the comfort of Christ
When he spake tenderly
    to his sorrowful flock:
The old words came to me
    by the riches of time
Mellow'd and transfigured
    as I stood on the hill
Heark'ning in the aspect
    of th' eternal silence.

THE OXEN

Christmas Eve, and twelve of the clock.
   "Now they are all on their knees,"
An elder said as we sat in a flock
   By the embers in hearthside ease.

We pictured the meek mild creatures where
   They dwelt in their strawy pen,
Nor did it occur to one of us there
   To doubt they were kneeling then.

So fair a fancy few would weave
   In these years! Yet, I feel,
If someone said on Christmas Eve,
   "Come; see the oxen kneel

"In the lonely barton by yonder coomb
   Our childhood used to know,"
I should go with him in the gloom,
   Hoping it might be so.

JEST 'FORE CHRISTMAS

Father calls me William, sister calls me Will,
Mother calls me Willie, but the fellers call me Bill!
Mighty glad I ain't a girl – ruther be a boy,
Without them sashes, curls, an' things that's worn
    by Fauntleroy!
Love to chawnk green apples an' go swimmin' in
    the lake –
Hate to take the castor-ile they give for bellyache!
'Most all the time, the whole year round, there ain't no
    flies on me,
But jest 'fore Christmas I'm as good as I kin be!

Got a yeller dog named Sport, sick him on the cat;
First thing she knows she does n't know where she
    is at!
Got a clipper sled, an' when us kids goes out to slide,
'Long comes the grocery cart, an' we all hook a ride!
But sometimes when the grocery man is worrited
    an' cross,
He reaches at us with his whip, an' larrups up his hoss,
An' then I laff an' holler, "Oh, ye never teched *me*!"
But jest 'fore Christmas I'm as good as I kin be!

Gran'ma says she hopes that when I git to be a man,
I'll be a missionarer like her oldest brother, Dan,

As was et up by the cannibuls that lives in
      Ceylon's Isle,
Where every prospeck pleases, an' only man is vile!
But gran'ma she has never been to see a Wild
      West show,
Nor read the Life of Daniel Boone, or else I guess
      she'd know
That Buff'lo Bill an' cowboys is good enough for me!
Excep' jest 'fore Christmas, when I'm good as
      I kin be!

And then old Sport he hangs around, so solemnlike
      an' still,
His eyes they seem a-sayin': "What's the matter,
      little Bill?"
The old cat sneaks down off her perch an' wonders
      what's become
Of them two enemies of hern that used to make
      things hum!
But I am so perlite an' tend so earnestly to biz,
That mother says to father: "How improved our
      Willie is!"
But father, havin' been a boy hisself, suspicions me
When, jest 'fore Christmas, I'm as good as I kin be!

For Christmas, with its lots an' lots of candies, cakes,
      an' toys,

Was made, they say, for proper kids an' not for
    naughty boys;
So wash yer face an' bresh yer hair, an' mind yer p's
    and q's,
An' don't bust out yer pantaloons, and don't wear out
    yer shoes;
Say "Yessum" to the ladies, and "Yessur" to the men,
An' when they's company, don't pass yer plate for
    pie again;
But, thinkin' of the things yer'd like to see upon
    that tree,
Jest 'fore Christmas be as good as yer kin be!

A VISIT FROM ST. NICHOLAS

'Twas the night before Christmas,
   when all through the house
Not a creature was stirring,
   not even a mouse;
The stockings were hung
   by the chimney with care,
In hopes that St. Nicholas
   soon would be there;

The children were nestled
   all snug in their beds,
While visions of sugar-plums
   danced through their heads;
And Mamma in her 'kerchief,
   and I in my cap,
Had just settled our brains
   for a long winter's nap,

When out on the lawn
   there arose such a clatter,
I sprang from my bed
   to see what was the matter.
Away to the window
   I flew like a flash,
Tore open the shutters
   and threw up the sash.

The moon on the breast
  of the new-fallen snow
Gave a lustre of mid-day
  to objects below,
When, what to my wondering
  eyes did appear,
But a miniature sleigh,
  and eight tiny rein-deer,

With a little old driver
  so lively and quick,
I knew in a moment
  he must be St. Nick.
More rapid than eagles
  his coursers they came,
And he whistled, and shouted,
  and called them by name:

"Now, Dasher! now, Dancer!
  now, Prancer and Vixen!
On, Comet! on, Cupid!
  on, Donder and Blixen!
To the top of the porch!
  to the top of the wall!
Now dash away! dash away!
  dash away, all!"

As leaves that before
    the wild hurricane fly,
When they meet with an obstacle,
    mount to the sky,
So up to the house-top
    the coursers they flew,
With the sleigh full of toys,
    and St. Nicholas too —

And then in a twinkling,
    I heard on the roof
The prancing and pawing
    of each little hoof.
As I drew in my head,
    and was turning around,
Down the chimney St. Nicholas
    came with a bound.

He was dressed all in fur,
    from his head to his foot,
And his clothes were all tarnished
    with ashes and soot;
A bundle of toys he had
    flung on his back,
And he looked like a peddler
    just opening his pack.

His eyes – how they twinkled!
   his dimples, how merry!
His cheeks were like roses,
   his nose like a cherry!
His droll little mouth
   was drawn up like a bow,
And the beard on his chin
   was as white as the snow;

The stump of a pipe
   he held tight in his teeth,
And the smoke it encircled
   his head like a wreath;
He had a broad face
   and a round little belly
That shook when he laughed,
   like a bowl full of jelly.

He was chubby and plump,
   a right jolly old elf,
And I laughed when I saw him
   in spite of myself;
A wink of his eye and
   a twist of his head
Soon gave me to know
   I had nothing to dread;

He spoke not a word, but
   went straight to his work,
And filled all the stockings;
   then turned with a jerk,
And laying his finger
   aside of his nose,
And giving a nod, up the
   chimney he rose.

He sprang to his sleigh,
   to his team gave a whistle,
And away they all flew
   like the down of a thistle.
But I heard him exclaim
   ere he drove out of sight –

"HAPPY CHRISTMAS TO ALL
   AND TO ALL A GOOD NIGHT!"

THE NATIVITY

UPON CHRIST HIS BIRTH

Strange news! a city full? will none give way
To lodge a guest that comes not every day?
No inn, nor tavern void? yet I descry
One empty place alone, where we may lie:
In too much fullness is some want: but where?
Men's empty hearts: let's ask for lodging there.
But if they not admit us, then we'll say
Their hearts, as well as inns, are made of clay.

ON THE MORNING OF CHRISTS NATIVITY

This is the Month, and this the happy morn
Wherin the Son of Heav'ns eternal King,
Of wedded Maid, and Virgin Mother born,
Our great redemption from above did bring;
For so the holy sages once did sing,
    That he our deadly forfeit should release,
And with his Father work us a perpetual peace.

That glorious Form, that Light unsufferable,
And that far-beaming blaze of Majesty,
Wherwith he wont at Heav'ns high Councel-Table,
To sit the midst of Trinal Unity,
He laid aside; and here with us to be,
    Forsook the Courts of everlasting Day,
And chose with us a darksom House of mortal Clay.

Say Heav'nly Muse, shall not thy sacred vein
Afford a present to the Infant God?
Hast thou no verse, no hymn, or solemn strein,
To welcom him to this his new abode,
Now while the Heav'n by the Suns team untrod,
    Hath took no print of the approaching light,
And all the spangled host keep watch in squadrons
        bright?

See how from far upon the Eastern rode
The Star-led Wisards haste with odours sweet,
O run, prevent them with thy humble ode,
And lay it lowly at his blessed feet;
Have thou the honour first, thy Lord to greet,
    And joyn thy voice unto the Angel Quire,
From out his secret Altar toucht with hallow'd fire.

The Hymn

It was the Winter wilde,
While the Heav'n-born-childe,
    All meanly wrapt in the rude manger lies;
Nature in aw to him
Had doff't her gawdy trim,
    With her great Master so to sympathize:
It was no season then for her
To wanton with the Sun her lusty Paramour.

Only with speeches fair
She woo's the gentle Air
    To hide her guilty front with innocent Snow,
And on her naked shame,
Pollute with sinfull blame,
    The Saintly Vail of Maiden white to throw,
Confounded, that her Makers eyes
Should look so neer upon her foul deformities.

But he her fears to cease,
Sent down the meek-eyd Peace,
   She crown'd with Olive green, came softly sliding
Down through the turning sphear
His ready Harbinger,
   With Turtle wing the amorous clouds dividing,
And waving wide her mirtle wand,
She strikes a universall Peace through Sea and Land.

No War, or Battails sound
Was heard the World around,
   The idle spear and shield were high up hung;
The hooked Chariot stood
Unstain'd with hostile blood,
   The Trumpet spake not to the armed throng,
And Kings sate still with awfull eye,
As if they surely knew their sovran Lord was by.

But peacefull was the night
Wherin the Prince of light
   His raign of peace upon the earth began:
The Windes with wonder whist,
Smoothly the waters kist,
   Whispering new joyes to the milde Ocean,
Who now hath quite forgot to rave,
While Birds of Calm sit brooding on the charmed wave.

The Stars with deep amaze
Stand fixt in stedfast gaze,
    Bending one way their pretious influence,
And will not take their flight,
For all the morning light,
    Or *Lucifer* that often warn'd them thence;
But in their glimmering Orbs did glow,
Untill their Lord himself bespake, and bid them go.

And though the shady gloom
Had given day her room,
    The Sun himself with-held his wonted speed,
And hid his head for shame,
As his inferiour flame,
    The new enlightn'd world no more should need;
He saw a greater Sun appear
Than his bright Throne, or burning Axletree could bear.

The Shepherds on the Lawn,
Or ere the point of dawn,
    Sate simply chatting in a rustick row;
Full little thought they than,
That the mighty *Pan*
    Was kindly com to live with them below;
Perhaps their loves, or els their sheep,
Was all that did their silly thoughts so busie keep.

When such musick sweet
Their hearts and ears did greet,
   As never was by mortall finger strook,
Divinely-warbled voice
Answering the stringed noise,
   As all their souls in blisfull rapture took:
The Air such pleasure loth to lose,
With thousand echo's still prolongs each heav'nly close.

Nature that heard such sound
Beneath the hollow round
   Of *Cynthia's* seat, the Airy region thrilling,
Now was almost won
To think her part was don,
   And that her raign had here its last fulfilling;
She knew such harmony alone
Could hold all Heav'n and Earth in happier union.

At last surrounds their sight
A Globe of circular light,
   That with long beams the shame-fac't night array'd,
The helmed Cherubim
And sworded Seraphim,
   Are seen in glittering ranks with wings displaid,
Harping in loud and solemn quire,
With unexpressive notes to Heav'ns new-born Heir.

Such Musick (as 'tis said)
Before was never made,
    But when of old the sons of morning sung,
While the Creator Great
His constellations set,
    And the well-ballanc't world on hinges hung,
And cast the dark foundations deep,
And bid the weltring waves their oozy channel keep.

Ring out ye Crystall sphears,
Once bless our human ears,
    (If ye have power to touch our senses so)
And let your silver chime
Move in melodious time;
    And let the Base of Heav'ns deep Organ blow,
And with your ninefold harmony
Make up full consort to th' Angelike symphony.

For if such holy Song
Enwrap our fancy long,
    Time will run back, and fetch the age of gold,
And speckl'd vanity
Will sicken soon and die,
    And leprous sin will melt from earthly mould,
And Hell it self will pass away,
And leave her dolorous mansions to the peering day.

Yea Truth, and Justice then
Will down return to men,
   Th' enameld *Arras* of the Rain-bow wearing,
And Mercy set between,
Thron'd in Celestiall sheen,
   With radiant feet the tissued clouds down stearing,
And Heav'n as at som festivall,
Will open wide the Gates of her high Palace Hall.

But wisest Fate sayes no,
This must not yet be so,
   The Babe lies yet in smiling Infancy,
That on the bitter cross
Must redeem our loss;
   So both himself and us to glorifie:
Yet first to those ychain'd in sleep,
The wakefull trump of doom must thunder through
     the deep,

With such a horrid clang
As on mount *Sinai* rang
   While the red fire, and smouldring clouds out brake:
The aged Earth agast
With terrour of that blast,
   Shall from the surface to the center shake;
When at the worlds last session,
The dreadfull Judge in middle Air shall spread his throne.

And then at last our bliss
Full and perfect is,
   But now begins; for from this happy day
Th' old Dragon under ground
In straiter limits bound,
   Not half so far casts his usurped sway,
And wrath to see his Kingdom fail,
Swindges the scaly Horrour of his foulded tail.

The Oracles are dumm,
No voice or hideous humm
   Runs through the arched roof in words deceiving.
Apollo from his shrine
Can no more divine,
   With hollow shreik the steep of *Delphos* leaving.
No nightly trance, or breathed spell,
Inspire's the pale-ey'd Priest from the prophetic cell.

The lonely mountains o're,
And the resounding shore,
   A voice of weeping heard, and loud lament;
From haunted spring, and dale
Edg'd with poplar pale,
   The parting Genius is with sighing sent,
With flowre-inwov'n tresses torn
The Nimphs in twilight shade of tangled thickets
     mourn.

In consecrated Earth,
And on the holy Hearth,
  The *Lars*, and *Lemures* moan with midnight plaint,
In Urns, and Altars round,
A drear, and dying sound
  Affrights the *Flamins* at their service quaint;
And the chill Marble seems to sweat,
While each peculiar power forgoes his wonted seat.

Peor, and *Baalim*,
Forsake their Temples dim,
  With that twice-batter'd god of *Palestine*,
And mooned *Ashtaroth*,
Heav'ns Queen and Mother both,
  Now sits not girt with Tapers holy shine,
The Libyc *Hammon* shrinks his horn,
In vain the *Tyrian* Maids their wounded *Thamuz*
      mourn.

And sullen *Moloch* fled,
Hath left in shadows dred,
  His burning Idol all of blackest hue,
In vain with Cymbals ring,
They call the grisly king,
  In dismall dance about the furnace blue;
The brutish gods of *Nile* as fast,
Isis and *Orus*, and the Dog *Anubis* hast.

Nor is *Osiris* seen
In *Memphian* Grove, or Green,
   Trampling the unshowr'd Grasse with lowings loud:
Nor can he be at rest
Within his sacred chest,
   Naught but profoundest Hell can be his shroud,
In vain with Timbrel'd Anthems dark
The sable-stoled Sorcerers bear his worshipt Ark.

He feels from *Juda's* Land
The dredded Infants hand,
   The rayes of *Bethlehem* blind his dusky eyn;
Nor all the gods beside,
Longer dare abide,
   Not *Typhon* huge ending in snaky twine:
Our Babe to shew his Godhead true,
Can in his swadling bands controul the damned crew.

So when the Sun in bed,
Curtain'd with cloudy red,
   Pillows his chin upon an Orient wave,
The flocking shadows pale,
Troop to th' infernall jail,
   Each fetter'd Ghost slips to his severall grave,
And the yellow-skirted *Fayes*,
Fly after the Night-steeds, leaving their Moon-lov'd
     maze.

But see the Virgin blest,
Hath laid her Babe to rest.
    Time is our tedious Song should here have ending,
Heav'ns youngest teemed Star,
Hath fixt her polisht Car,
    Her sleeping Lord with Handmaid Lamp attending:
And all about the Courtly Stable,
Bright-harnest Angels sit in order serviceable.

NATIVITY

Immensity cloistered in thy dear womb,
Now leaves his well-beloved imprisonment,
There he hath made himself to his intent
Weak enough, now into our world to come;
But Oh, for thee, for him, hath th' Inn no room?
Yet lay him in this stall, and from the Orient,
Stars, and wisemen will travel to prevent
Th' effect of Herod's jealous general doom.
Seest thou, my Soul, with thy faith's eyes, how he
Which fills all place, yet none holds him, doth lie?
Was not his pity towards thee wondrous high,
That would have need to be pitied by thee?
Kiss him, and with him into Egypt go,
With his kind mother, who partakes thy woe.

THE NATIVITY
Written in the year 1656

Peace? and to all the world? sure, one
And he the prince of peace, hath none.
He travels to be born, and then
Is born to travel more agen.
Poor *Galile!* thou can'st not be
The place for his Nativity.
His restless mother's call'd away,
And not deliver'd till she pay.

    A *Tax?* 'tis so still! we can see
The Church thrive in her misery;
And like her head at *Bethlem*, rise
When she opprest with troubles, lyes.
Rise? should all fall, we cannot be
In more extremities than he.
Great *Type* of passions! come what will,
Thy grief exceeds all *copies* still.
Thou cam'st from heav'n to earth, that we
Might go from Earth to Heav'n with thee.
And though thou found'st no welcom here,
Thou did'st provide us *mansions* there.
A *stable* was thy *Court*, and when
Men turn'd to *beasts*; Beasts would be *Men*.
They were thy *Courtiers*, others none;
And their poor *Manger* was thy *Throne*.

No swadling *silks* thy Limbs did fold,
Though thou could'st turn thy Rays to gold.
No *Rockers* waited on thy birth,
No *Cradles* stirr'd: nor songs of mirth;
But her chast *Lap* and sacred *Brest*
Which lodg'd thee first, did give thee *rest*.
   But stay: what light is that doth stream,
And drop here in a gilded beam?
It is thy Star runs *page*, and brings
Thy tributary *Eastern* Kings.
Lord! grant some *Light* to us, that we
May with them find the way to thee.
Behold what mists eclipse the day:
How dark it is! shed down one *Ray*
To guide us out of this sad night,
And say once more, *Let there be Light.*

NEW PRINCE, NEW POMP

Behold, a silly tender Babe
    In freezing winter night
In homely manger trembling lies,
    Alas, a piteous sight!

The inns are full; no man will yield
    This little pilgrim bed,
But forced he is with silly beasts
    In crib to shroud his head.

Despise him not for lying there,
    First, what he is inquire;
An orient pearl is often found
    In depth of dirty mire.

Weigh not his crib, his wooden dish,
    Nor beasts that by him feed;
Weigh not his Mother's poor attire,
    Nor Joseph's simple weed.

This stable is a Prince's court,
    This crib his chair of state;
The beasts are parcel of his pomp,
    The wooden dish his plate.

The persons in that poor attire
    His royal liveries wear;
The Prince himself is come from heaven;
    This pomp is prized there.

With joy approach, O Christian wight,
    Do homage to thy King;
And highly praise his humble pomp,
    Which he from heaven doth bring.

THE NATIVITY OF OUR LORD
AND SAVIOUR JESUS CHRIST

Where is this stupendous stranger?
    Swains of Solyma, advise;
Lead me to my Master's manger,
    Shew me where my Saviour lies.

O Most Mighty! O Most Holy!
    Far beyond the seraph's thought,
Art thou then so mean and lowly
    As unheeded prophets taught?

O the magnitude of meekness!
    Worth from worth immortal sprung;
O the strength of infant weakness,
    If eternal is so young!

If so young and thus eternal,
    Michael tune the shepherd's reed,
Where the scenes are ever vernal,
    And the loves be love indeed!

See the God blasphem'd and doubted
    In the schools of Greece and Rome;
See the pow'rs of darkness routed,
    Taken at their utmost gloom.

Nature's decorations glisten
    Far above their usual trim;
Birds on box and laurels listen,
    As so near the cherubs hymn.

Boreas now no longer winters
    On the desolated coast;
Oaks no more are riv'n in splinters
    By the whirlwind and his host.

Spinks and ouzles sing sublimely,
    "We too have a Saviour born";
Whiter blossoms burst untimely
    On the blest Mosaic thorn.

God all-bounteous, all-creative,
    Whom no ills from good dissuade,
Is incarnate, and a native
    Of the very world he made.

FOR THE NATIVITY

Shepherds, I sing you, this winter's night
Our Hope new-planted, the womb'd, the buried Seed:
For a strange Star has fallen, to blossom from a tomb,
And infinite Godhead circumscribed, hangs helpless
    at the breast.

Now the cold airs are musical, and all the ways of
    the sky
Vivid with moving fires, above the hills where tread
The feet – how beautiful! – of them that publish peace.

The sacrifice, which is not made for them,
The angels comprehend, and bend to earth
Their worshipping way. Material kind Earth
Gives Him a Mother's breast, and needful food.

A Love, shepherds, most poor,
And yet most royal, kings,
Begins this winter's night;
But oh, cast forth, and with no proper place,
Out in the cold He lies!

CHRISTMAS

A child is born, they cry, a child
And he is Noble and not Mild
(It is the child that makes them wild)

The King sits brooding on his throne
He looks around and calls a man:
My men bring me a heavy stone.

My men bring me a purple robe
And bring me whips and iron goad.
They brought them to him where he strode.

My men bring gold and bring incense
And fetch all noble children at once
That I shall never take offence.

The men fetched the noble children away
They lifted them up and cried: Hurray.
The King sat back and clapped their play.

All noble mild children are brought home
To the wicked King who has cast them down
And ground their bones on the heavy stone.

But the child that is Noble and not Mild
He lies in his cot. He is unbeguiled.
He is Noble, he is not Mild,
And he is born to make men wild.

THE MAID-SERVANT AT THE INN

"It's queer," she said; "I see the light
    As plain as I beheld it then,
All silver-like and calm and bright –
    We've not had stars like that again!

"And she was such a gentle thing
    To birth a baby in the cold.
The barn was dark and frightening –
    This new one's better than the old.

"I mind my eyes were full of tears,
    For I was young, and quick distressed,
But she was less than me in years
    That held a son against her breast.

"I never saw a sweeter child –
    The little one, the darling one! –
I mind I told her, when he smiled
    You'd know he was his mother's son.

"It's queer that I should see them so –
    The time they came to Bethlehem
Was more than thirty years ago;
    I've prayed that all is well with them."

JOSEPH

If the stars fell; night's nameless dreams
    Of bliss and blasphemy came true,
If skies were green and snow were gold,
    And you loved me as I love you;

O long light hands and curled brown hair,
    And eyes where sits a naked soul;
Dare I even then draw near and burn
    My fingers in the aureole?

Yes, in the one wise foolish hour
    God gives this strange strength to a man.
He can demand, though not deserve,
    Where ask he cannot, seize he can.

But once the blood's wild wedding o'er,
    Were not dread his, half dark desire,
To see the Christ-child in the cot,
    The Virgin Mary by the fire?

THE MOTHER OF GOD

The threefold terror of love; a fallen flare
Through the hollow of an ear;
Wings beating about the room;
The terror of all terrors that I bore
The Heavens in my womb.

Had I not found content among the shows
Every common woman knows,
Chimney corner, garden walk,
Or rocky cistern where we tread the clothes
And gather all the talk?

What is this flesh I purchased with my pains,
This fallen star my milk sustains,
This love that makes my heart's blood stop
Or strikes a sudden chill into my bones
And bids my hair stand up?

SHEPHERD'S SONG
AT CHRISTMAS

Look there at the star!
I, among the least,
Will arise and take
A journey to the East.
But what shall I bring
As a present for the King?
What shall I bring to the Manger?

      I will bring a song,
      A song that I will sing,
      A song for the King
      In the Manger.

Watch out for my flocks,
Do not let them stray.
I am going on a journey
Far, far away.
But what shall I bring
As a present for the Child?
What shall I bring to the Manger?

      I will bring a lamb,
      Gentle, meek, and mild,
      A lamb for the Child
      In the Manger.

I'm just a shepherd boy,
Very poor I am –
But I know there is
A King in Bethlehem.
What shall I bring
As a present just for Him?
What shall I bring to the Manger?

I will bring my heart
And give my heart to Him.
I will bring my heart
To the Manger.

THE THREE KINGS

Three Kings came riding from far away,
   Melchior and Gaspar and Baltasar;
Three Wise Men out of the East were they,
And they travelled by night and they slept by day,
   For their guide was a beautiful, wonderful star.

The star was so beautiful, large, and clear,
   That all the other stars of the sky
Became a white mist in the atmosphere,
And by this they knew that the coming was near
   Of the Prince foretold in the prophecy.

Three caskets they bore on their saddle-bows,
   Three caskets of gold with golden keys;
Their robes were of crimson silk with rows
Of bells and pomegranates and furbelows,
   Their turbans like blossoming almond-trees.

And so the Three Kings rode into the West,
   Through the dusk of night, over hill and dell,
And sometimes they nodded with beard on breast,
And sometimes talked, as they paused to rest,
   With the people they met at some wayside well.

"Of the child that is born," said Baltasar,
   "Good people, I pray you, tell us the news;
For we in the East have seen his star,
And have ridden fast, and have ridden far,
   To find and worship the King of the Jews."

And the people answered, "You ask in vain;
   We know of no king but Herod the Great!"
They thought the Wise Men were men insane,
As they spurred their horses across the plain,
   Like riders in haste, and who cannot wait.

And when they came to Jerusalem,
   Herod the Great, who had heard this thing,
Sent for the Wise Men and questioned them;
And said, "Go down unto Bethlehem,
   And bring me tidings of this new king."

So they rode away; and the star stood still,
   The only one in the gray of morn;
Yes, it stopped, – it stood still of its own free will,
Right over Bethlehem on the hill,
   The city of David, where Christ was born.

And the Three Kings rode through the gate and the guard,
    Through the silent street, till their horses turned
And neighed as they entered the great inn-yard;
But the windows were closed, and the doors
        were barred,
    And only a light in the stable burned.

And cradled there in the scented hay,
    In the air made sweet by the breath of kine,
The little child in the manger lay,
The child, that would be king one day
    Of a kingdom not human but divine.

His mother Mary of Nazareth
    Sat watching beside his place of rest,
Watching the even flow of his breath,
For the joy of life and the terror of death
    Were mingled together in her breast.

They laid their offerings at his feet:
    The gold was their tribute to a King,
The frankincense, with its odor sweet,
Was for the Priest, the Paraclete,
    The myrhh for the body's burying.

And the mother wondered and bowed her head,
    And sat as still as a statue of stone;

Her heart was troubled yet comforted,
Remembering what the Angel had said
   Of an endless reign and of David's throne.

Then the Kings rode out of the city gate,
   With a clatter of hoofs in proud array;
But they went not back to Herod the Great
For they knew his malice and feared his hate,
   And returned to their homes by another way.

JOURNEY OF THE MAGI

"A cold coming we had of it,
Just the worst time of the year
For a journey, and such a long journey:
The ways deep and the weather sharp,
The very dead of winter."
And the camels galled, sore-footed, refractory,
Lying down in the melting snow.
There were times we regretted
The summer palaces on slopes, the terraces,
And the silken girls bringing sherbet.
Then the camel men cursing and grumbling
And running away, and wanting their liquor and
        women,
And the night-fires going out, and the lack
        of shelters,
And the cities hostile and the towns unfriendly
And the villages dirty and charging high prices:
A hard time we had of it.
At the end we preferred to travel all night,
Sleeping in snatches,
With the voices singing in our ears, saying
That this was all folly.

Then at dawn we came down to a temperate valley,
Wet, below the snow line, smelling of vegetation;

With a running stream and a water-mill beating
        the darkness,
And three trees on the low sky,
And an old white horse galloped away in the meadow.
Then we came to a tavern with vine-leaves over
        the lintel,
Six hands at an open door dicing for pieces of silver,
And feet kicking the empty wine-skins.
But there was no information, and so we continued
And arrived at evening, not a moment too soon
Finding the place; it was (you may say) satisfactory.

All this was a long time ago, I remember,
And I would do it again, but set down
This set down
This: were we led all that way for
Birth or Death? There was a Birth, certainly,
We had evidence and no doubt. I had seen birth
        and death,
But had thought they were different; this Birth was
Hard and bitter agony for us, like Death, our death.
We returned to our places, these Kingdoms,
But no longer at ease here, in the old dispensation,
With an alien people clutching their gods.
I should be glad of another death.

THE ADORATION OF THE KINGS

From the Nativity
which I have already celebrated
the Babe in its Mother's arms

the Wise Men in their stolen
splendor
and Joseph and the soldiery

attendant
with their incredulous faces
make a scene copied we'll say

from the Italian masters
but with a difference
the mastery

of the painting
and the mind the resourceful mind
that governed the whole

the alert mind dissatisfied with
what it is asked to
and cannot do

accepted the story and painted
it in the brilliant
colors of the chronicler

the downcast eyes of the Virgin
as a work of art
for profound worship

THE THREE HOLY KINGS
Legend

Once long ago when at the desert's edge
the Lord's hand spread open –
as if a fruit should deep in summer
proclaim its seed –
there was a miracle: across
vast distances a constellation formed
out of three kings and a star.

Three kings from On-the-Way
and the star Everywhere,
who all pushed on (just think!)
to the right a Rex and the left a Rex
toward a silent stall.

What was there that they *didn't* bring
to that stall of Bethlehem!
Each step clanked out ahead of them,
as the one who rode the sable horse
sat plush and velvet-snug.
And the one who walked upon his right
was like some man of gold,
and the one who sauntered on his left
with sling and swing
and jang and jing

from a round silver thing
that hung swaying inside rings,
began to smoke deep blue.
Then the star Everywhere laughed
so strangely over them,
and ran ahead and found the stall
and said to Mary:
I am bringing here an errantry
made up of many strangers.
Three kings with ancient might
heavy with gold and topaz
and dark, dim, and heathenish, –
but don't you be afraid.
They have all three at home
twelve daughters, not one son,
so they'll ask for use of yours
as sunshine for their heaven's blue
and comfort for their throne.
Yet don't straightaway believe: merely
some sparkle-prince and heathen-sheik
is to be your young son's lot.
Consider: the road is long.
They've wandered far, like herdsmen,
and meanwhile their ripe empire falls

into the lap of Lord knows whom.
And while here, warmly like westwind,
the ox snorts into their ear,
they are perhaps already destitute
and headless, for all they know.
So with your smile cast light
on that confusion which they are,
and turn your countenance
toward dawning with your child:
there in blue lines lies
what each one left for you:
Emeralda and Rubinien
and the Valley of Turquoise.

CAROL OF THE
THREE KINGS

How long ago we dreamed
Evening and the human
Step in the quiet groves
And the prayer we said:
Walk upon the darkness,
Words of the lord,
Contain the night, the dead
And here comfort us.
We have been a shadow
Many nights moving,
Swaying many nights
Between yes and no.
We have been blindness
Between sun and moon
Coaxing the time
For a doubtful star.
Now we cease, we forget
Our reasons, our city,
The sun, the perplexed day,
Noon, the irksome labor,
The flushed dream, the way,
Even the dark beasts,
Even our shadows.
In this night and day

All gifts are nothing:
What is frankincense
Where all sweetness is?
We that were followers
In the night's confusion
Kneel and forget our feet
Who the cold way came.
Now in the darkness
After the deep song
Walk among the branches
Angels of the lord,
Over earth and child
Quiet the boughs.
Now shall we sing or pray?
Where has the night gone?
Who remembers day?
We are breath and human
And awake have seen
All birth and burial
Merge and fall away,
Seen heaven that extends
To comfort all the night,
We have felt morning move
The grove of a few hands.

CHRISTMASTIDE

THE MASQUE OF CHRISTMAS

Now God preserve, as you well do deserve,
    Your majesties all two there;
Your highness small, with my good lords all,
    And ladies, how do you do there?

Give me leave to ask, for I bring you a masque
    From little, little, little London;
Which say the king likes, I have passed the pikes,
    If not, old Christmas is undone.

Our dance's freight is a matter of eight,
    And two, the which are wenches:
In all they be ten, four cocks to a hen,
    And will swim to the tune like tenches.

Each hath his knight for to carry his light,
    Which some would say are torches;
To bring them here, and to lead them there,
    And home again to their own porches.

Now their intent, is above to present,
    With all the appurtenances,
A right Christmas, as of old it was,
    To be gathered out of the dances.

Which they do bring, and afore the king,
    The queen, and prince, as it were now
Drawn here by love; who over and above,
    Doth draw himself in the gear too.

Hum drum, sauce for a coney;
    No more of your martial music;
Even for the sake o' the next new stake,
    For there I do mean to use it.

And now to ye, who in place are to see,
    With roll and farthingale hoopéd:
I pray you know, though he want his bow,
    By the wings, that this is Cupid.

He might go back for to cry, What you lack?
    But that were not so witty:
His cap and coat are enough to note,
    That he is the Love o' the city.

And he leads on, though he now be gone,
    For that was only his-rule:
But now comes in, Tom of Bosoms-inn,
    And he presenteth Mis-rule.

Which you may know, by the very show,
    Albeit you never ask it:

For there you may see, what his ensigns be,
  The rope, the cheese, and the basket.

This Carol plays, and has been in his days
  A chirping boy, and a kill-pot:
Kit cobbler it is, I'm a father of his,
  And he dwells in the lane call'd Fill-pot.

But who is this? O, my daughter Cis,
  Minced-pie; with her do not dally
On pain o' your life: she's an honest cook's wife,
  And comes out of Scalding Alley.

Next in the trace, comes Gambol in place:
  And, to make my tale the shorter,
My son Hercules, ta'en out of Distaff Lane,
  But an active man, and a porter.

Now Post and Pair, old Christmas's heir,
  Doth make and a jingling sally;
And wot you who, 'tis one of my two
  Sons, card-makers in Pur Alley.

Next in a trice, with his box and his dice,
  Mac'-pipin my son, but younger,
Brings Mumming in; and the knave will win,
  For he is a costermonger.

But New Year's Gift, of himself makes shift,
    To tell you what his name is:
With orange on head, and his ginger-bread,
    Clem Wasp of Honey Lane 'tis.

This, I you tell, is our jolly Wassel,
    And for Twelfth-night more meet too:
She works by the ell, and her name is Nell,
    And she dwells in Threadneedle Street too.

Then Offering, he, with his dish and his tree,
    That in every great house keepeth,
Is by my son, young Little-worth, done,
    And in Penny-rich Street he sleepeth.

Last, Baby-cake, that an end doth make
    Of Christmas' merry, merry vein-a,
Is child Rowlan, and a straight young man,
    Though he come out of Crooked Lane-a.

There should have been, and a dozen I ween,
    But I could find but one more
Child of Christmas, and a Log it was,
    When I them all had gone o'er.

I prayéd him, in a time so trim,
    That he would make one to prance it:
And I myself would have been the twelfth,
    O but Log was too heavy to dance it.

THE TRUE CHRISTMAS

So stick up *Ivie* and the *Bays*,
And then restore the *heathen* ways.
Green will remind you of the spring,
Though this great day denies the thing.
And mortifies the Earth and all
But your wild *Revels*, and loose *Hall*.
Could you wear *Flow'rs*, and *Roses* strow
Blushing upon your breasts *warm Snow*,
That very *dress* your lightness will
Rebuke, and wither at the Ill.
The brightness of this day we owe
Not unto *Music*, *Masque* nor *Showe*:
Nor gallant *furniture*, nor *Plate*;
But to the *Manger's* mean Estate.
His *life* while here, as well as *birth*,
Was but a check to *pomp* and *mirth*;
And all mans *greatness* you may see
Condemn'd by his *humility*.

   Then leave your open *house* and *noise*,
To welcom him with *holy Joys*,
And the poor *Shepherd's* watchfulness:
Whom *light* and *hymns* from Heav'n did bless.
What you *abound* with, cast abroad
To those that *want*, and ease your loade.
Who empties thus, will bring more in;

But riot is both *loss* and *Sin*.
Dress finely what comes not in sight,
And then you keep your *Christmas* right.

OLD CHRISTMASTIDE

Heap on more wood! – the wind is chill;
But let it whistle as it will,
We'll keep our Christmas merry still.
Each age has deemed the new-born year
The fittest time for festal cheer.
Even heathen yet, the savage Dane
At Iol more deep the mead did drain;
High on the beach his galley drew,
And feasted all his pirate crew;
Then in his low and pine-built hall,
Where shields and axes decked the wall,
They gorged upon the half-dressed steer;
Caroused in seas of sable beer;
While round, in brutal jest, were thrown
The half-gnawed rib and marrow-bone,
Or listened all, in grim delight,
While scalds yelled out the joy of fight,
Then forth in frenzy would they hie,
While wildly loose their red locks fly;
And, dancing round the blazing pile,
They make such barbarous mirth the while,
As best might to the mind recall
The boisterous joys of Odin's hall.
And well our Christian sire of old
Loved when the year its course had rolled,

And brought blithe Christmas back again,
With all his hospitable train.
Domestic and religious rite
Gave honour to the holy night:
On Christmas eve the bells were rung;
On Christmas eve the mass was sung;
That only night, in all the year,
Saw the stoled priest the chalice rear.
The damsel donned her kirtle sheen;
The hall was dressed with holly green;
Forth to the wood did merry men go,
To gather in the mistletoe;
Then opened wide the baron's hall
To vassal, tenant, serf, and all;
Power laid his rod of rule aside,
And ceremony doffed his pride.
The heir, with roses in his shoes,
That night might village partner choose;
The lord, underogating, share
The vulgar game of "post and pair."
All hailed, with uncontrolled delight,
And general voice, the happy night
That to the cottage, as the crown,
Brought tidings of salvation down.
The fire, with well-dried logs supplied,
Went roaring up the chimney wide;
The huge hall-table's oaken face,

Scrubbed till it shone, the day to grace,
Bore then upon its massive board
No mark to part the squire and lord.
Then was brought in the lusty brawn
By old blue-coated serving man;
Then the grim boar's head frowned on high,
Crested with bays and rosemary.
Well can the green-garbed ranger tell,
How, when, and where the monster fell;
What dogs before his death he tore,
And all the baiting of the boar.
The Wassail round, in good brown bowls,
Garnished with ribbons, blithely trowls.
There the huge sirloin reeked; hard by
Plum-porridge stood, and Christmas pie;
Nor failed old Scotland to produce,
At such high tide, her savoury goose.
Then came the merry masquers in,
And carols roared with blithesome din;
If unmelodious was the song,
It was a hearty note, and strong,
Who lists may in their mumming see
Traces of ancient mystery;
White shirts supplied the masquerade,
And smutted cheeks the vizors made:
But, what masquers, richly dight,
Can boast of bosoms half so light?

England was merry England, when
Old Christmas brought his sports again.
'Twas Christmas broached the mightiest ale;
'Twas Christmas told the merriest tale;
A Christmas gambol oft could cheer
The poor man's heart through half the year.

CHRISTMAS AT SEA

The sheets were frozen hard, and they cut the naked
    hand;
The decks were like a slide, where a seaman scarce
    could stand;
The wind was a nor'wester, blowing squally off the sea;
And cliffs and spouting breakers were the only things
    a-lee.

They heard the surf a-roaring before the break of day;
But 'twas only with the peep of light we saw how ill
    we lay.
We tumbled every hand on deck instanter, with a shout,
And we gave her the maintops'l, and stood by to go
    about.
All day we tacked and tacked between the South Head
    and the North;
All day we hauled the frozen sheets, and got no further
    forth;
All day as cold as charity, in bitter pain and dread,
For very life and nature we tacked from head to head.

We gave the South a wider berth, for there the tide-
    race roared;
But every tack we made we brought the North Head
    close aboard;

So 's we saw the cliffs and houses, and the breakers
    running high,
And the coastguard in his garden, with his glass
    against his eye.

The frost was on the village roofs as white as ocean
    foam;
The good red fires were burning bright in every
    'longshore home;
The windows sparkled clear, and the chimneys
    volleyed out;
And I vow we sniffed the victuals as the vessel went
    about.

The bells upon the church were rung with a mighty
    jovial cheer;
For it's just that I should tell you how (of all days in the
    year)
This day of our adversity was blessèd Christmas morn,
And the house above the coastguard's was the house
    where I was born.

O well I saw the pleasant room, the pleasant faces
    there,
My mother's silver spectacles, my father's silver hair;
And well I saw the firelight, like a flight of homely
    elves,

Go dancing round the china-plates that stand upon the
     shelves.

And well I knew the talk they had, the talk that was
          of me,
Of the shadow on the household and the son that went
          to sea;
And O the wicked fool I seemed, in every kind of way,
To be here and hauling frozen ropes on blessèd
          Christmas Day.

They lit the high sea-light, and the dark began to fall.
"All hands to loose topgallant sails," I heard the
          captain call.
"By the Lord, she'll never stand it," our first mate,
          Jackson, cried.
... "It's the one way or the other, Mr. Jackson," he
          replied.

She staggered to her bearings, but the sails were new
          and good,
And the ship smelt up to windward just as though she
          understood.
As the winter's day was ending, in the entry of the
          night,
We cleared the weary headland, and passed below
          the light.

And they heaved a mighty breath, every soul on board
    but me,
As they saw her nose again pointing handsome out
    to sea;
But all that I could think of, in the darkness and the
    cold,
Was just that I was leaving home and my folks were
    growing old.

THE CHRISTMAS TREE

Put out the lights now!
Look at the Tree, the rough tree dazzled
In oriole plumes of flame,
Tinselled with twinkling frost fire, tasselled
With stars and moons – the same
That yesterday hid in the spinney and had no fame
Till we put out the lights now.

Hard are the nights now:
The fields at moonrise turn to agate,
Shadows are cold as jet;
In dyke and furrow, in copse and faggot
The frost's tooth is set;
And stars are the sparks whirled out by the north
        wind's fret
On the flinty nights now.

So feast your eyes now
On mimic star and moon-cold bauble:
Worlds may wither unseen,
But the Christmas Tree is a tree of fable,
A phoenix in evergreen,
And the world cannot change or chill what its
        mysteries mean
To your hearts and eyes now.

The vision dies now
Candle by candle: the tree that embraced it
Returns to its own kind,
To be earthed again and weather as best it
May the frost and the wind.
Children, it too had its hour – you will not mind
If it lives or dies now.

OUR CHRISTMAS TREE

Our Christmas tree is
not electrified, is not
covered with little lights
calling attention to themselves
(we have had enough
of little lights calling attention
to themselves). Our tree
is a cedar cut here, one
of the fragrances of our place,
hung with painted cones
and paper stars folded
long ago to praise our tree,
Christ come into the world.

DECEMBER

Glad Christmas comes, and every hearth
    Makes room to give him welcome now,
E'en want will dry its tears in mirth,
    And crown him with a holly bough;
Though tramping 'neath a winter sky,
    O'er snowy paths and rimy stiles,
The housewife sets her spinning by
    To bid him welcome with her smiles.

Each house is swept the day before,
    And windows stuck with ever-greens,
The snow is besom'd from the door,
    And comfort crowns the cottage scenes.
Gilt holly, with its thorny pricks,
    And yew and box, with berries small,
These deck the unused candlesticks,
    And pictures hanging by the wall.

Neighbours resume their annual cheer,
    Wishing, with smiles and spirits high,
Glad Christmas and a happy year,
    To every morning passer-by;
Milkmaids their Christmas journeys go,
    Accompanied with favour'd swain;
And children pace the crumping snow,
    To taste their granny's cake again.

The shepherd, now no more afraid,
    Since custom doth the chance bestow,
Starts up to kiss the giggling maid
    Beneath the branch of misletoe
That 'neath each cottage beam is seen,
    With pearl-like berries shining gay;
The shadow still of what hath been,
    Which fashion yearly fades away.

The singing wates, a merry throng,
    At early morn, with simple skill,
Yet imitate the angels song,
    And chant their Christmas ditty still;
And, 'mid the storm that dies and swells
    By fits – in hummings softly steals
The music of the village bells,
    Ringing round their merry peals.

When this is past, a merry crew,
    Bedeck'd in masks and ribbons gay,
The "Morris-dance," their sports renew,
    And act their winter evening play.
The clown turn'd king, for penny-praise,
    Storms with the actor's strut and swell;
And Harlequin, a laugh to raise,
    Wears his hunch-back and tinkling bell.

And oft for pence and spicy ale,
	With winter nosegays pinn'd before,
The wassail-singer tells her tale,
	And drawls her Christmas carols o'er.
While 'prentice boy, with ruddy face,
	And rime-bepowder'd, dancing locks,
From door to door with happy pace,
	Runs round to claim his "Christmas box."

The block upon the fire is put,
	To sanction custom's old desires;
And many a fagot's bands are cut,
	For the old farmers' Christmas fires;
Where loud-tongued Gladness joins the throng,
	And Winter meets the warmth of May,
Till feeling soon the heat too strong,
	He rubs his shins, and draws away.

While snows the window-panes bedim,
	The fire curls up a sunny charm,
Where, creaming o'er the pitcher's rim,
	The flowering ale is set to warm;
Mirth, full of joy as summer bees,
	Sits there, its pleasures to impart,
And children, 'tween their parent's knees,
	Sing scraps of carols o'er by heart.

And some, to view the winter weathers,
  Climb up the window-seat with glee,
Likening the snow to falling feathers,
  In Fancy's infant ecstasy;
Laughing, with superstitious love,
  O'er visions wild that youth supplies,
Of people pulling geese above,
  And keeping Christmas in the skies.

As tho' the homestead trees were drest,
  In lieu of snow, with dancing leaves;
As tho' the sun-dried martin's nest,
  Instead of i'cles hung the eaves;
The children hail the happy day –
  As if the snow were April's grass,
And pleas'd, as 'neath the warmth of May,
  Sport o'er the water froze to glass.

Thou day of happy sound and mirth,
  That long with childish memory stays,
How blest around the cottage hearth
  I met thee in my younger days!
Harping, with rapture's dreaming joys,
  On presents which thy coming found,
The welcome sight of little toys,
  The Christmas gift of cousins round.

The wooden horse with arching head,
    Drawn upon wheels around the room;
The gilded coach of gingerbread,
    And many-colour'd sugar plum;
Gilt cover'd books for pictures sought,
    Or stories childhood loves to tell,
With many an urgent promise bought,
    To get to-morrow's lesson well.

And many a thing, a minute's sport,
    Left broken on the sanded floor,
When we would leave our play, and court
    Our parents' promises for more.
Tho' manhood bids such raptures die,
    And throws such toys aside as vain,
Yet memory loves to turn her eye,
    And count past pleasures o'er again.

Around the glowing hearth at night,
    The harmless laugh and winter tale
Go round, while parting friends delight
    To toast each other o'er their ale;
The cotter oft with quiet zeal
    Will musing o'er his Bible lean;
While in the dark the lovers steal
    To kiss and toy behind the screen.

Old customs! Oh! I love the sound,
    However simple they may be:
Whate'er with time hath sanction found,
    Is welcome, and is dear to me.
Pride grows above simplicity,
    And spurns them from her haughty mind,
And soon the poet's song will be
    The only refuge they can find.

MEDITATIONS ON CHRISTMAS

CHRISTMAS

All after pleasures as I rid one day,
   My horse and I, both tir'd, bodie and minde,
   With full crie of affections, quite astray,
I took up in the next inne I could finde.
There when I came, whom found I but my deare,
   My dearest Lord, expecting till the grief
   Of pleasures brought me to him, readie there
To be all passengers most sweet relief?
O Thou, whose glorious, yet contracted light,
   Wrapt in nights mantle, stole into a manger;
   Since my dark soul and brutish is thy right,
To Man of all beasts be not thou a stranger:
   Furnish & deck my soul, that thou mayst have
   A better lodging then a rack or grave.

The shepherds sing; and shall I silent be?
           My God, no hymne for thee?
My soul's a shepherd too; a flock it feeds
           Of thoughts, and words, and deeds.
The pasture is thy word: the streams, thy grace
           Enriching all the place.
Shepherd and flock shall sing, and all my powers
           Out-sing the day-light houres.
Then we will chide the sunne for letting night
           Take up his place and right:

We sing one common Lord; wherefore he should
            Himself the candle hold.
I will go searching, till I find a sunne
            Shall stay, till we have done;
A willing shiner, that shall shine as gladly,
            As frost-nipt sunnes look sadly.
Then we will sing, and shine all our own day,
            And one another pay:
His beams shall cheer my breast, and both so twine,
Till ev'n his beams sing, and my musick shine.

THE BURNING BABE

As I in hoary Winter's night stood shiveringe in the
    snowe,
Surpris'd I was with sodayne heat, which made my hart
    to glowe;
And lifting upp a fearfull eye to vewe what fire was
    nere,
A prety Babe all burninge bright, did in the ayre
    appeare,
Who scorchèd with excessive heate, such floodes of
    teares did shedd,
As though His floodes should quench His flames which
    with His teares were fedd;
Alas! quoth He, but newly borne, in fiery heates I frye,
Yet none approach to warme their hartes or feele my
    fire but I!
My faultles brest the fornace is, the fuell woundinge
    thornes,
Love is the fire, and sighes the smoke, the ashes shame
    and scornes;
The fuell Justice layeth on, and Mercy blowes the
    coales,
The mettall in this fornace wrought are men's defilèd
    soules,
For which, as nowe on fire I am, to worke them to their
    good,

So will I melt into a bath to washe them in My bloode:
With this He vanisht out of sight, and swiftly shroncke
     awaye,
And straight I callèd unto mynde that it was
     Christmas-daye.

THE SAVIOR MUST
HAVE BEEN A DOCILE GENTLEMAN

The Savior must have been
A docile Gentleman –
To come so far so cold a Day
For little Fellowmen –

The Road to Bethlehem
Since He and I were Boys
Was leveled, but for that 'twould be
A rugged billion Miles –

A CHRISTMAS HYMN

> *And some of the Pharisees from among the*
> *multitude said unto him, Master, rebuke thy*
> *disciples.*
> *And he answered and said unto them, I*
> *tell you that, if these should hold their peace,*
> *the stones would immediately cry out.*
> — *St. Luke XIX. 39–40*

A stable-lamp is lighted
Whose glow shall wake the sky;
The stars shall bend their voices,
And every stone shall cry.
And every stone shall cry,
And straw like gold shall shine;
A barn shall harbor heaven,
A stall become a shrine.

This child through David's city
Shall ride in triumph by;
The palm shall strew its branches,
And every stone shall cry.
And every stone shall cry,
Though heavy, dull, and dumb,
And lie within the roadway
To pave his kingdom come.

Yet he shall be forsaken,
And yielded up to die;
The sky shall groan and darken,
And every stone shall cry.
And every stone shall cry
For stony hearts of men:
God's blood upon the spearhead,
God's love refused again.

But now, as at the ending,
The low is lifted high;
The stars shall bend their voices,
And every stone shall cry.
And every stone shall cry
In praises of the child
By whose descent among us
The worlds are reconciled.

CHRISTMAS

They say: but cattle near
And the infant in harsh hay!
Indeed harsh: how could honest God
Be man another way?

By lying lax in gold
Near many a bent knee?
Bedded in bright percent and so
Vouching hypocrisy?

Oh man's-flesh is most really this:
A thin cry in the cold;
Dust made a little while aware,
Shriveled both young and old.

When infants are born rich
The gaudy zoos troop in:
The elephant with button eyes;
The tiger, springs of tin.

And friends and relatives gape,
A simple clucking clan.
More honest – no? – when Bethlehem
Told the home-truth of man.

SONNETS AT CHRISTMAS

I

This is the day His hour of life draws near,
Let me get ready from head to foot for it
Most handily with eyes to pick the year
For small feed to reward a feathered wit.
Some men would see it an epiphany
At ease, at food and drink, others at chase;
Yet I, stung lassitude, with ecstasy
Unspent argue the season's difficult case
So: Man, dull creature of enormous head,
What would he look at in the coiling sky?
But I must kneel again unto the Dead
While Christmas bells of paper white and red,
Figured with boys and girls spilt from a sled,
Ring out the silence I am nourished by.

II

Ah, Christ, I love you rings to the wild sky
And I must think a little of the past:
When I was ten I told a stinking lie
That got a black boy whipped; but now at last
The going years, caught in an after-glow,
Reverse like balls englished upon green baize –
Let them return, let the round trumpets blow
The ancient crackle of the Christ's deep gaze.

Deafened and blind, with senses yet unfound,
Am I, untutored to the after-wit
Of knowledge, knowing a nightmare has no sound;
Therefore with idle hands and head I sit
In late December before the fire's daze
Punished by crimes of which I would be quit.

AN OLD SONG ENDED
at Christmas

All earthly pomp or beauty to express
  Is but to carve in snow, on waves to write.
Celestial things, though men conceive them less,
  Yet fullest are they in themselves of light;
Such beams they yield as know no means to die,
Such heat they cast as lifts the spirit high.

Your tire tracks have spoiled the snow outside,
  And inside, where there's something wrong,
    the stem's
Corrupt but slick subtext is magnified
  In the vase beneath a Star of Bethlehem.
If nature disappoints, as it appears,
Whom do we trust when each the other fears?

Where once the stars had crossed themselves to light
  A way for kings, or show as angels to the boy
Minding his flock, who stares to see the night
  All changed into a story quick with joy,
Now is nothing but fire, nothing but air.
The only pattern here's this view, this chair.

It's difficult to look for long at snow,
  When most of heaven's fallen to earth out there.

A scalding brilliance poured over the cold.
    Trees, the road, your car – lost in the glare.
To steep myself in light, then close my eyes . . .
Those winter days are darkness in disguise.

But here you come, bursting in the door,
    Sunlight and snowlight streaming in behind.
Is blindness, then, the gift you give before
    The rest? – forgiveness, say, so hard to find
In what's at hand, the common day which seems
At last the light that yields such heat, such beams.

A CHRISTMAS POEM
Written for the 1982 Carol Service
of Nene College, Northampton

One of the oxen said
"I know him, he is me – a beast
  Of burden, used, abused,
  Excluded from the feast –
  A toiler, one by whom
  No task will be refused:
I wish him strength, I give him room."

One of the shepherds said
"I know him, he is me – a man
  Who wakes when others sleep,
  Whose watchful eyes will scan
  The drifted snow at night
  Alert for the lost sheep:
I give this lamb, I wish him sight."

One of the wise men said
"I know him, he is me – a king
  On wisdom's pilgrimage,
  One Plato claimed would bring
  The world back to its old
  Unclouded golden age:
I wish him truth, I give him gold."

Mary his mother said
"I know his heart's need, it is mine –
    The chosen child who lives
    Lost in his Lord's design,
    The self and symbol of
    The selfless life he gives:
I give him life, I wish him love."

ILLUMINATION

Ground lapis for the sky, and scrolls of gold,
Before which shepherds kneel, gazing aloft
At visiting angels clothed in egg-yolk gowns,
Celestial tinctures smuggled from the East,
From sunlit Eden, the palmed and plotted banks
Of sun-tanned Aden. Brought home in fragile grails,
Planted in England, rising at Eastertide,
Their petals cup stamens of topaz dust,
The powdery stuff of cooks and cosmeticians.
But to the camels-hair tip of the finest brush
Of Brother Anselm, it is the light of dawn,
Gilding the hems, the sleeves, the fluted pleats
Of the antiphonal archangelic choirs
Singing their melismatic *pax in terram.*
The child lies cribbed below, in bestial dark,
Pale as the tiny tips of crocuses
That will find their way to the light through drifts
         of snow.

CHRISTMAS
CRACKERS

THE MAHOGANY TREE

Christmas is here:
Winds whistle shrill.
Icy and chill:
Little care we.
Little we fear
Weather without,
Sheltered about
The Mahogany Tree.

Commoner greens,
Ivy and oaks,
Poets, in jokes,
Sing, do you see:
Good fellows' shins
Here, boys, are found,
Twisting around
The Mahogany Tree.

Once on the boughs
Birds of rare plume
Sang, in its bloom:
Night birds are we;
Here we carouse,
Singing, like them,
Perched round the stem
Of the jolly old tree.

Here let us sport,
Boys, as we sit:
Laughter and wit
Flashing so free.
Life is but short –
When we are gone,
Let them sing on,
Round the old tree.

Evenings we knew,
Happy as this;
Faces we miss,
Pleasant to see.
Kind hearts and true,
Gentle and just,
Peace to your dust!
We sing round the tree.

Care, like a dun,
Lurks at the gate:
Let the dog wait;
Happy we'll be!
Drink every one;
Pile up the coals,
Fill the red bowls,
Round the old tree!

Drain we the cup. –
Friend, art afraid?
Spirits are laid
In the Red Sea.
Mantle it up;
Empty it yet;
Let us forget,
Round the old tree.

Sorrows, begone!
Life and its ills,
Duns and their bills,
Bid we to flee.
Come with the dawn
Blue-devil sprite,
Leave us to-night,
Round the old tree.

CHRISTMAS

The bells of waiting Advent ring,
    The Tortoise stove is lit again
And lamp-oil light across the night
    Has caught the streaks of winter rain
In many a stained-glass window sheen
From Crimson Lake to Hooker's Green.

The holly in the windy hedge
    And round the Manor House the yew
Will soon be stripped to deck the ledge,
    The altar, font and arch and pew,
So that the villagers can say
"The church looks nice" on Christmas Day.

Provincial public houses blaze
    And Corporation tramcars clang,
On lighted tenements I gaze
    Where paper decorations hang,
And bunting in the red Town Hall
Says "Merry Christmas to you all."

And London shops on Christmas Eve
    Are strung with silver bells and flowers
As hurrying clerks the City leave

To pigeon-haunted classic towers,
And marbled clouds go scudding by
The many-steepled London sky.

And girls in slacks remember Dad,
    And oafish louts remember Mum,
And sleepless children's hearts are glad,
    And Christmas-morning bells say "Come!"
Even to shining ones who dwell
Safe in the Dorchester Hotel.

And is it true? And is it true,
    This most tremendous tale of all,
Seen in a stained-glass window's hue,
    A Baby in an ox's stall?
The Maker of the stars and sea
Become a Child on earth for me?

And is it true? For if it is,
    No loving fingers tying strings
Around those tissued fripperies,
    The sweet and silly Christmas things,
Bath salts and inexpensive scent
And hideous tie so kindly meant,

No love that in a family dwells,
    No carolling in frosty air,
Nor all the steeple-shaking bells
    Can with this single Truth compare –
That God was Man in Palestine
And lives to-day in Bread and Wine.

THE DARK CHRISTMAS
ON WILDWOOD ROAD

'Twas Christmas Eve and bitter cold;
The west wind raked the frozen mold,
And flaws of snow, with scorpion whips,
Picked at a myriad weather strips,
And scourged the lated reveller
In dream-enfolded Westchester.

And in the house on Wildwood Road
The unattended furnace glowed
And dimmed to ashen gray. Thereat
The punctual-fingered thermostat
Growled a command to draft and lever.
The furnace fire was out, however.

Out of the baleful midnight shine,
A little sour with early wine,
Mouthing the dregs of Christmas glee,
Came Mrs. D. and Mr. D.

"You'll have to fix the furnace, dear!"
Said she. He sought a wounding sneer,
And then disdained to answer thus
The obvious with the obvious.

He cleaned the ash-pit with a frown,
With savage strokes he shook her down,
He found behind the fruit-room door
A box full of excelsior;
He found some scraps of barrel-staving,
A broken chair his wife was saving.
He dribbled coal with skillful care.
Then, sleep-befuddled, climbed the stair.

And very early Christmas morn
Junior blew his Christmas horn,
And Mrs. D said cheerily:
"A merry Christmas, Mr. D!"
She dressed in rapid negligée
To fetch the gifts of Christmas Day;
But soon returned, a dread surmise
Swimming in amazèd eyes.

"Oh did you see, behind the door,
A box full of excelsior,
Containing, in its tangled mass,
A goblet of Bohemian glass?
Oh tell me that you did not throw –"

"Well, how the hell was I to know?"

"Oh, what a senseless thing to do!
The present I was giving you!
It was a strange and dusky red,
A masterpiece, the salesman said.
You burned my present up!"

                      "Oh, come,
It seems to me a little dumb
To leave such things around where someone
Can burn them up!"

                  "So, I'm the dumb one!
Because I wanted to surprise you!
And *I'm* to blame! Oh, I despise you!
I sometimes wish I'd not been born!"
And Junior blew his Christmas horn.

The unrepentant furnace glowed
In the little house on Wildwood Road.
Thermostatically controlled,
The drafts checkmated heat and cold.
What thermostat can regulate
The heart in sorrow and in hate?

And all that red-eyed Christmas morn
Junior blew his clamorous horn.

LADY SELECTING HER CHRISTMAS CARDS

Fastidiously, with gloved and careful fingers,
   Through the marked samples she pursues her search.
Which shall it be: the snowscape's wintry languors
   Complete with church,

An urban skyline, children sweetly pretty
   Sledding downhill, the chaste, ubiquitous wreath,
Schooner or candle or the simple Scottie
   With verse underneath?

Perhaps it might be better to emblazon
   With words alone the stiff, punctilious square.
(Oh, not Victorian, certainly. This season
   One meets it everywhere.)

She has a duty proper to the weather —
   A Birth she must announce, a rumor to spread,
Wherefore the very spheres once sang together
   And a star shone overhead.

Here are the Tidings which the shepherds panted
   One to another, kneeling by their flocks.
And they will bear her name (engraved, not printed),
   Twelve-fifty for the box.

PHYLLIS McGINLEY   139

CITY CHRISTMAS

Now is the time when the great urban heart
  More warmly beats, exiling melancholy.
Turkey comes table d'hôte or à la carte.
  Our elevator wears a wreath of holly.

Mendicant Santa Claus in flannel robes
  At every corner contradicts his label,
Alms-asking. We've a tree with colored globes
  In our apartment foyer, on a table.

There is a promise – or a threat – of snow
  Noised by the press. We pull our collars tighter.
And twenty thousand doormen hourly grow
  Politer and politer and politer.

OFFICE PARTY

This holy night in open forum
   Miss McIntosh, who handles Files,
Has lost one shoe and her decorum.
   Stately, the frozen chairman smiles

On Media, desperately vocal.
   Credit, though they have lost their hopes
Of edging toward an early Local,
   Finger their bonus envelopes.

The glassy boys, the bursting girls
   Of Copy, start a Conga clatter
To a swung carol. Limply curls
   The final sandwich on the platter

Till hark! a herald Messenger
   (Room 414) lifts loudly up
His quavering tenor. Salesmen stir
   Libation for his Lily cup.

"Noel," he pipes, "Noel, Noel."
   Some wag beats tempo with a ruler.
And the plump blonde from Personnel
   Collapses by the water cooler.

CHRISTMAS IRONIES

CHRISTMAS IS COMING

Darkness is for the poor, and thorough cold,
As they go wandering the hills at night,
Gunning for enemies. Winter locks the lake;
The rocks are harder for it. What was grass
Is fossilized and brittle; it can hurt,
Being a torture to the kneeling knee,
And in the general pain of cold, it sticks
Particular pain where crawling is required.

> *Christmas is coming. The goose is getting fat.*
> *Please put a penny in the Old Man's hat.*

Where is the warmth of blood? The enemy
Has ears that can hear clearly in the cold,
Can hear the shattering of fossil grass,
Can hear the stiff cloth rub against itself,
Making a sound. Where is the blood? It lies
Locked in the limbs of some poor animal
In a diaspora of crimson ice.
The skin freezes to metal. One must crawl
Quietly in the dark. Where is the warmth?
The lamb has yielded up its fleece and warmth
And woolly life, but who shall taste of it?
Here on the ground one cannot see the stars.
The lamb is killed. *The goose is getting fat.*

A wind blows steadily against the trees,
And somewhere in the blackness they are black.
Yet crawling one encounters bits of string,
Pieces of foil left by the enemy.
(A rifle takes its temper from the cold.)
Where is the pain? The sense has frozen up,
And fingers cannot recognize the grass,
Cannot distinguish their own character,
Being blind with cold, being stiffened by the cold;
Must find out thistles to remember pain.
Keep to the frozen ground or else be killed.
Yet crawling one encounters in the dark
The frosty carcasses of birds, their feet
And wings all glazed. And still we crawl to learn
Where pain was lost, how to recover pain.
Reach for the brambles, crawl to them and reach,
Clutching for thorns, search carefully to feel
The point of thorns, life's crown, *the Old Man's hat.*
Yet quietly. Do not disturb the brambles.
Winter has taught the air to clarify
All noises, and the enemy can hear
Perfectly in the cold. Nothing but sound
Is known. Where is the warmth and pain?
Christmas is coming. Darkness is for the poor.

> *If you haven't got a penny, a ha'penny will do,*
> *If you haven't got a ha'penny, God bless you.*

THE HOUSE OF CHRISTMAS

There fared a mother driven forth
Out of an inn to roam;
In the place where she was homeless
All men are at home.
The crazy stable close at hand,
With shaking timber and shifting sand,
Grew a stronger thing to abide and stand
Than the square stones of Rome.

For men are homesick in their homes,
And strangers under the sun,
And they lay their heads in a foreign land
Whenever the day is done.
Here we have battle and blazing eyes,
And chance and honour and high surprise,
But our homes are under miraculous skies
Where the yule tale was begun.

A Child in a foul stable,
Where the beasts feed and foam;
Only where He was homeless
Are you and I at home;
We have hands that fashion and heads that know,
But our hearts we lost – how long ago!
In a place no chart nor ship can show
Under the sky's dome.

This world is wild as an old wives' tale,
And strange the plain things are,
The earth is enough and the air is enough
For our wonder and our war;
But our rest is as far as the fire-drake swings
And our peace is put in impossible things
Where clashed and thundered unthinkable wings
Round an incredible star.

To an open house in the evening
Home shall men come,
To an older place than Eden
And a taller town than Rome.
To the end of the way of the wandering star,
To the things that cannot be and that are,
To the place where God was homeless
And all men are at home.

CHRISTMAS BELLS

I heard the bells on Christmas Day
Their old, familiar carols play,
    And wild and sweet
    The words repeat
Of peace on earth, good-will to men!

And thought how, as the day had come,
The belfries of all Christendom
    Had rolled along
    The unbroken song
Of peace on earth, good-will to men!

Till, ringing, singing on its way,
The world revolved from night to day,
    A voice, a chime
    A chant sublime
Of peace on earth, good-will to men!

Then from each black, accursed mouth
The cannon thundered in the South,
    And with the sound
    The carols drowned
Of peace on earth, good-will to men!

It was as if an earthquake rent
The hearth-stones of a continent,
    And made forlorn
    The households born
Of peace on earth, good-will to men!

And in despair I bowed my head;
"There is no peace on earth," I said;
    "For hate is strong,
    And mocks the song
Of peace on earth, good-will to men!"

Then pealed the bells more loud and deep:
"God is not dead; nor doth he sleep!
    The Wrong shall fail,
    The Right prevail,
With peace on earth, good-will to men!"

A NATIVITY
1914–18

The Babe was laid in the Manger
  Between the gentle kine –
All safe from cold and danger –
    "But it was not so with mine,
              (With mine! With mine!)
"Is it well with the child, is it well?"
    The waiting mother prayed.
"For I know not how he fell,
    And I know not where he is laid."

A Star stood forth in Heaven;
  The Watchers ran to see
The Sign of the Promise given –
    "But there comes no sign to me.
              (To me! To me!)
"*My* child died in the dark.
    Is it well with the child, is it well?
There was none to tend him or mark,
    And I know not how he fell."

The Cross was raised on high;
  The Mother grieved beside –
"But the Mother saw Him die
    And took Him when He died.
              (He died! He died!)

"Seemly and undefiled
    His burial-place was made –
Is it well, is it well with the child?
    For I know not where he is laid."

On the dawning of Easter Day
    Comes Mary Magdalene;
But the Stone was rolled away,
    And the Body was not within –
                (Within! Within!)
"Ah, who will answer my word?"
    The broken mother prayed.
"They have taken away my Lord,
    And I know not where He is Laid."

"The Star stands forth in Heaven.
    The watchers watch in vain
For Sign of the Promise given
    Of peace on Earth again –
                (Again! Again!)
"But I know for Whom he fell" –
    The steadfast mother smiled,
"Is it well with the child – is it well?
    It is well – it is well with the child!"

CHRISTMAS TREES

Bonhoeffer in his skylit cell
bleached by the flares' candescent fall,
pacing out his own citadel,

restores the broken themes of praise,
encourages our borrowed days,
by logic of his sacrifice.

Against wild reasons of the state
his words are quiet but not too quiet.
We hear too late or not too late.

GEOFFREY HILL

A CHRISTMAS CARD, AFTER THE ASSASSINATIONS

What is to be born already fidgets in the stem,
near where the old leaves loosened, resembling them,
or burns in the cell, ready to be blue-eyed,
or, in the gassy heavens, gathers toward a solid,
except for that baby mutant, Christ or beast,
who forms himself from a wish, our best or last.

CHRISTMAS IN BIAFRA (1969)

This sunken-eyed moment wobbling
down the rocky steepness on broken
bones slowly fearfully to hideous
concourse of gathering sorrows in the valley
will yet become in another year a lost
Christmas irretrievable in the heights
its exploding inferno transmuted
by cosmic distances to the peacefulness
of a cool twinkling star . . . To death-cells
of that moment came faraway sounds of other
men's carols floating on crackling waves
mocking us. With regret? Hope? Longing? None of
these, strangely, not even despair rather
distilling pure transcendental hate . . .

Beyond the hospital gate
the good nuns had set up a manger
of palms to house a fine plastercast
scene at Bethlehem. The Holy
Family was central, serene, the Child
Jesus plump wise-looking and rose-cheeked; one
of the magi in keeping with legend
a black Othello in sumptuous robes. Other
figures of men and angels stood
at well-appointed distances from

the heart of the divine miracle
and the usual cattle gazed on
in holy wonder . . .

Poorer than the poor worshippers
before her who had paid their homage
with pitiful offering of new aluminium
coins that few traders would take and
a frayed five-shilling note she only
crossed herself and prayed open-eyed. Her
infant son flat like a dead lizard
on her shoulder his arms and legs
cauterized by famine was a miracle
of its kind. Large sunken eyes
stricken past boredom to a flat
unrecognizing glueyiness moped faraway
motionless across her shoulder . . .

Now her adoration over
she turned him around and pointed
at those pretty figures of God
and angels and men and beasts –
a spectacle to stir the heart
of a child. But all he vouchsafed
was one slow deadpan look of total
unrecognition and he began again
to swivel his enormous head away

to mope as before at his empty distance . . .
She shrugged her shoulders, crossed
herself again and took him away.

A CHRISTMAS GHOST-STORY
Christmas-eve 1899

South of the Line, inland from far Durban,
A mouldering soldier lies – your countryman.
Awry and doubled up are his gray bones,
And on the breeze his puzzled phantom moans
Nightly to clear Canopus: "I would know
By whom and when the All-Earth-gladdening Law
Of Peace, brought in by that Man Crucified,
Was ruled to be inept, and set aside?
And what of logic or of truth appears
In tacking 'Anno Domini' to the years?
Near twenty-hundred liveried thus have hied,
But tarries yet the Cause for which He died."

CHRISTMAS IN INDIA

Dim dawn behind the tamarisks – the sky is saffron-
    yellow –
  As the women in the village grind the corn,
And the parrots seek the river-side, each calling to his
    fellow
    That the Day, the staring Eastern Day, is born.
      O the white dust on the highway! O the stenches
        in the byway!
        O the clammy fog that hovers over earth!
      And at Home they're making merry 'neath the
        white and scarlet berry –
        What part have India's exiles in their mirth?

Full day behind the tamarisks – the sky is blue and
    staring –
  As the cattle crawl afield beneath the yoke,
And they bear One o'er the field-path, who is past all
    hope or caring,
    To the ghat below the curling wreaths of smoke.
      Call on Rama, going slowly, as ye bear a brother
        lowly –
        Call on Rama – he may hear, perhaps, your voice!
      With our hymn-books and our psalters we appeal
        to other altars,
        And to-day we bid "good Christian men rejoice!"

High noon behind the tamarisks – the sun is hot
    above us –
  As at Home the Christmas Day is breaking wan.
They will drink our healths at dinner – those who tell
    us how they love us,
    And forget us till another year be gone!
      O the toil that knows no breaking! O the *heimweh*,
        ceaseless, aching!
        O the black dividing Sea and alien Plain!
        Youth was cheap – wherefore we sold it. Gold was
        good – we hoped to hold it.
        And to-day we know the fulness of our gain!

Grey dusk behind the tamarisks – the parrots fly
    together –
  As the Sun is sinking slowly over Home;
And his last ray seems to mock us shackled in a lifelong
    tether
  That drags us back howe'er so far we roam.
      Hard her service, poor her payment – she is
        ancient, tattered raiment –
        India, she the grim Stepmother of our kind.
      If a year of life be lent her, if her temple's shrine
        we enter,
        The door is shut – we may not look behind.

Black night behind the tamarisks – the owls begin
    their chorus –
  As the conches from the temple scream and bray.
With the fruitless years behind us and the hopeless
    years before us,
  Let us honour, O my brothers, Christmas Day!
    Call a truce, then, to our labours – let us feast with
        friends and neighbours,
      And be merry as the custom of our caste;
    For, if "faint and forced the laughter," and if
        sadness follow after,
      We are richer by one mocking Christmas past.

A CHRISTMAS SONNET

For One in Doubt

While you that in your sorrow disavow
Service and hope, see love and brotherhood
Far off as ever, it will do no good
For you to wear his thorns upon your brow
For doubt of him. And should you question how
To serve him best, he might say, if he could,
"Whether or not the cross was made of wood
Whereon you nailed me, is no matter now."

Though other saviors have in older lore
A Legend, and for older gods have died –
Though death may wear the crown it always wore
And ignorance be still the sword of pride –
Something is here that was not here before,
And strangely has not yet been crucified.

A CAROL

Oh hush thee, my baby,
Thy cradle's in pawn:
No blankets to cover thee
Cold and forlorn.
The stars in the bright sky
Look down and are dumb
At the heir of the ages
Asleep in a slum.

The hooters are blowing,
No heed let him take;
When baby is hungry
'Tis best not to wake.
Thy mother is crying,
Thy dad's on the dole:
Two shillings a week is
The price of a soul.

THE CHRISTMAS ROBIN

The snows of February had buried Christmas
Deep in the woods, where grew self-seeded
The fir-trees of a Christmas yet unknown,
Without a candle or a strand of tinsel.

Nevertheless when, hand in hand, plodding
Between the frozen ruts, we lovers paused
And "Christmas trees!" cried suddenly together,
Christmas was there again, as in December.

We velveted our love with fantasy
Down a long vista-row of Christmas trees,
Whose coloured candles slowly guttered down
As grandchildren came trooping round our knees.

But he knew better, did the Christmas robin –
The murderous robin with his breast aglow
And legs apart, in a spade-handle perched:
He prophesied more snow, and worse than snow.

CHRISTMAS SONGS AND CAROLS

CAROL

I sing the birth was born to-night,
The author both of life and light;
   The angels so did sound it,
And, like the ravished shepherds said,
Who saw the light, and were afraid,
   Yet searched, and true they found it.

The Son of God, the eternal king,
That did us all salvation bring,
   And freed our soul from danger,
He whom the whole world could not take,
The Word, which heaven and earth did make,
   Was now laid in a manger.

The Father's wisdom willed it so,
The Son's obedience knew no No;
   Both wills were in one stature,
And, as that wisdom had decreed,
The Word was now made flesh indeed,
   And took on him our nature.

What comfort by him we do win,
Who made himself the price of sin,
   To make us heirs of glory!
To see this babe, all innocence,
A martyr born in our defence,
   Can man forget the story?

BEN JONSON

AN ODE OF THE BIRTH
OF OUR SAVIOUR

In Numbers, and but these few,
I sing Thy Birth, Oh JESU!
Thou prettie Babie, borne here,
With sup'rabundant scorn here:
Who for Thy Princely Port here,
   Hadst for Thy place
   Of Birth, a base
Out-stable for thy Court here.

Instead of neat Inclosures
Of inter-woven Osiers;
Instead of fragrant Posies
Of Daffadills, and Roses;
Thy cradle, Kingly Stranger,
   As Gospell tells,
   Was nothing els,
But, here, a homely manger.

But we with Silks, (not Cruells)
With sundry precious Jewells,
And Lilly-work will dresse Thee;
And as we dispossesse thee
Of clouts, wee'l make a chamber,
   Sweet Babe, for Thee,

Of Ivorie,
And plaister'd round with Amber.

The Jewes they did disdaine Thee,
But we will entertaine Thee
With Glories to await here
Upon Thy Princely State here,
And more for love, then pittie.
From yeere to yeere
Wee'l make Thee, here,
A Free-born of our Citie.

ON CHRISTMAS DAY TO MY HEART

To Day:
Hark! Heaven sings!
Stretch, tune my Heart
(For hearts have strings
May bear their part)
And though thy Lute were bruis'd i' th' fall;
Bruis'd hearts may reach an humble Partoral.

To Day
Shepheards rejoyce
And Angells do
No more: thy voice
Can reach that too:
Bring then at least thy pipe along
And mingle Consort with the Angells Song.

To Day
A shed that's thatch'd
(Yet straws can sing)
Holds God; God's match'd
With beasts; Beasts bring
Their song their way; For shame then raise
Thy notes; Lambs bleat and Oxen bellow Praise.

To Day
God honour'd Man
Not Angells: Yet
They sing; And can
Rais'd Man forget?
Praise is our debt to-day, nor shall
Angells (Man's not so poor) discharge it all.

To Day
Then screwe thee high
My Heart: Up to
The Angells key;
Sing Glory; Do;
What if thy stringes all crack and flye?
On such a Ground, Musick 'twill be to dy.

A CHRISTMAS CAROL

The shepherds went their hasty way,
   And found the lowly stable-shed
Where the virgin-mother lay:
   And now they checked their eager tread,
For to the babe, that at her bosom clung,
A mother's song the virgin-mother sung.

They told her how a glorious light,
   Streaming from a heavenly throng,
Around them shone, suspending night;
   While sweeter than a mother's song,
Blessed angels heralded the Saviour's birth,
Glory to God on high! and peace on earth.

She listened to the tale divine,
   And closer still the babe she pressed;
And while she cried, "The babe is mine!"
   The milk rushed faster to her breast:
Joy rose within her, like a summer's morn:
Peace, peace on earth! the Prince of peace is born.

Thou mother of the Prince of peace,
   Poor, simple, and of low estate;
That strife should vanish, battle cease,

Oh! why should this thy soul elate?
Sweet music's loudest note, the poet's story,
Didst thou ne'er love to hear of fame and glory?

And is not War a youthful king,
    A stately hero clad in mail?
Beneath his footsteps laurels spring;
    Him earth's majestic monarchs hail!
Their friend, their playmate! and his bold bright eye
Compels the maiden's love-confessing sigh.

"Tell this in some more courtly scene,
    To maids and youths in robes of state!
I am a woman poor and mean,
    And therefore is my soul elate.
War is a ruffian, all with guilt defiled,
That from the aged father tears his child!

"A murderous fiend, by fiends adored,
    He kills the sire and starves the son,
The husband kills, and from her board
    Steals all his widow's toil had won;
Plunders God's world of beauty; rends away
All safety from the night, all comfort from the day.

"Then wisely is my soul elate,
    That strife should vanish, battle cease;
I'm poor, and of a low estate,
    The mother of the Prince of peace!
Joy rises in me, like a summer's morn;
Peace, peace on earth! the Prince of peace is born!"

From IN MEMORIAM

CVI

Ring out, wild bells, to the wild sky,
    The flying cloud, the frosty light:
    The year is dying in the night;
Ring out, wild bells, and let him die.

Ring out the old, ring in the new,
    Ring, happy bells, across the snow:
    The year is going, let him go;
Ring out the false, ring in the true.

Ring out the grief that saps the mind,
    For those that here we see no more;
    Ring out the feud of rich and poor,
Ring in redress to all mankind.

Ring out a slowly dying cause,
    And ancient forms of party strife;
    Ring in the nobler modes of life,
With sweeter manners, purer laws.

Ring out the want, the care, the sin,
    The faithless coldness of the times;
    Ring out, ring out my mournful rhymes,
But ring the fuller minstrel in.

Ring out false pride in place and blood,
    The civic slander and the spite;
    Ring in the love of truth and right;
Ring in the common love of good.

Ring out old shapes of foul disease;
    Ring out the narrowing lust of gold;
    Ring out the thousand wars of old,
Ring in the thousand years of peace.

Ring in the valiant man and free,
    The larger heart, the kindlier hand;
    Ring out the darkness of the land,
Ring in the Christ that is to be.

FRENCH NOEL

Masters, in this Hall,
    Hear ye news to-day
Brought from over sea,
    And ever I you pray.

Nowell! Nowell! Nowell! Nowell sing we clear
Holpen are all folk on earth, Born is God's Son so dear:
Nowell! Nowell! Nowell! Nowell sing we loud!
God to-day hath poor folk rais'd, And cast down the proud.

Going over the hills,
    Through the milk-white snow,
Heard I ewes bleat
    While the wind did blow.

Shepherds many an one
    Sat among the sheep,
No man spake more word
    Than they had been asleep.

Quoth I "Fellows mine,
    Why this guise sit ye?
Making but dull cheer,
    Shepherds though ye be?

"Shepherds should of right
  Leap and dance and sing;
Thus to see ye sit
  Is a right strange thing."

Quoth these fellows then,
  "To Bethlem town we go,
To see a mighty Lord
  Lie in a manger low."

"How name ye this Lord,
  Shepherds?" then said I.
"Very *God*," they said,
  "Come from Heaven high."

Then to Bethlem town
  We went two and two
And in a sorry place
  Heard the oxen low.

Therein did we see
  A sweet and goodly May
And a fair old man;
  Upon the straw She lay.

And a little Child
  On Her arm had She;

"Wot ye Who this is?"
  Said the hinds to me.

Ox and ass Him know,
  Kneeling on their knee:
Wondrous joy had I
  This little Babe to see.

This is Christ the Lord
  Masters, be ye glad!
Christmas is come in,
  And no folk should be sad.

Nowell! Nowell! Nowell! Nowell sing we clear
Holpen are all folk on earth, Born is God's Son so dear:
Nowell! Nowell! Nowell! Nowell sing we loud!
God to-day hath poor folk rais'd, And cast down the proud.

CHRISTUS NATUS EST

In Bethlehem
On Christmas morn,
The lowly gem
Of love was born.
Hosannah! *Christus natus est.*

Bright in her crown
Of fiery star,
Judea's town
Shone from afar:
Hosannah! *Christus natus est.*

While beasts in stall,
On bended knee,
Did carol all
Most joyously:
Hosannah! *Christus natus est.*

For bird and beast
He did not come,
But for the least
Of mortal scum.
Hosannah! *Christus natus est.*

Who lies in ditch?
Who begs his bread?
Who has no stitch
For back or head?
Hosannah! *Christus natus est.*

Who wakes to weep,
Lies down to mourn?
Who in his sleep
Withdraws from scorn?
Hosannah! *Christus natus est.*

Ye outraged dust,
On field and plain,
To feed the lust
Of madmen slain:
Hosannah! *Christus natus est.*

The manger still
Outshines the throne;
Christ must and will
Come to his own.
Hosannah! *Christus natus est.*

COUNTEE CULLEN

A CAROL

The warmth of cows
    That chewed on hay
And cherubim
Protected Him
    As small He lay.

Chickens and sheep
    Knew He was there
Because all night
A holy light
    Suffused the air.

Darkness was long
    And the sun brief
When the Child arose
A man of sorrows
    And friend to grief.

A LULLABY

Lullee, lullay,
I could not love thee more
If thou wast Christ the King.
Now tell me, how did Mary know
That in her womb should sleep and grow
The Lord of everything?

Lullee, lullay,
An angel stood with her
Who said, "That which doth stir
Like summer in thy side
Shall save the world from sin.
Then stable, hall and inn
Shall cherish Christmas-tide."

Lullee, lullay,
And so it was that Day.
And did she love Him more
Because an angel came
To prophesy His name?
Ah no, not so,
She could not love Him more,
But loved Him just the same.
Lullee, lullee, lullay.

JANET LEWIS   183

WHILE SHEPHERDS WATCHED
THEIR FLOCKS BY NIGHT

While shepherds watched their flocks by night,
    All seated on the ground,
The angel of the Lord came down,
    And glory shone around.

Fear not! said he; for mighty dread
    Had seized their troubled mind:
Glad tidings of great joy I bring
    To you and all mankind.

To you, in David's town, this day
    Is born, of David's line,
A Saviour, who is Christ the Lord;
    And this shall be the sign:

The heavenly Babe you there shall find
    To human view displayed,
All meanly wrapped in swaddling bands
    And in a manger laid.

Thus spake the seraph; and forthwith
    Appeared a shining throng
Of angels praising God, and thus
    Addressed their joyful song:

All glory be to God on high,
    And to the earth be peace;
Good will henceforth from heaven to men
    Begin and never cease!

NAHUM TATE

GOOD KING WENCESLAS

Good King Wenceslas looked out,
    On the Feast of Stephen,
When the snow lay round about,
    Deep, and crisp, and even:
Brightly shone the moon that night,
    Though the frost was cruel,
When a poor man came in sight,
    Gathering winter fuel.

"Hither, page, and stand by me,
    If thou know'st it, telling,
Yonder peasant, who is he?
    Where and what his dwelling?"
"Sire, he lives a good league hence,
    Underneath the mountain,
Right against the forest fence,
    By Saint Agnes' fountain."

"Bring me flesh, and bring me wine,
    Bring me pine-logs hither:
Thou and I will see him dine,
    When we bear them thither."
Page and monarch, forth they went,
    Forth they went together;
Through the rude wind's wild lament
    And the bitter weather.

"Sire, the night is darker now,
    And the wind blows stronger;
Fails my heart, I know not how;
    I can go no longer."
"Mark my footsteps, good my page;
    Tread thou in them boldly:
Thou shalt find the winter's rage
    Freeze thy blood less coldly."

In his master's steps he trod,
    Where the snow lay dinted;
Heat was in the very sod
    Which the Saint had printed.
Therefore, Christian men, be sure,
    Wealth or rank possessing,
Ye who now will bless the poor,
    Shall yourselves find blessing.

J. M. NEALE

O LITTLE TOWN OF BETHLEHEM

O little town of Bethlehem,
  How still we see thee lie!
Above thy deep and dreamless sleep
  The silent stars go by.
Yet in thy dark streets shineth
  The everlasting light;
The hopes and fears of all the years
  Are met in thee to-night.

O morning stars, together
  Proclaim the holy birth,
And praises sing to God the King,
  And peace to men on earth;
For Christ is born of Mary;
  And, gathered all above,
While mortals sleep, the angels keep
  Their watch of wondering love.

How silently, how silently,
  The wondrous gift is given!
So God imparts to human hearts
  The blessings of his heaven.
No ear may hear his coming;
  But in this world of sin,
Where meek souls will receive him, still
  The dear Christ enters in.

Where children pure and happy
　Pray to the blessèd Child,
Where misery cries out to thee,
　Son of the mother mild;
Where charity stands watching
　And faith holds wide the door,
The dark night wakes, the glory breaks,
　And Christmas comes once more.

O holy Child of Bethlehem,
　Descend to us, we pray;
Cast out our sin, and enter in,
　Be born in us to-day.
We hear the Christmas Angels
　The great glad tidings tell:
O come to us, abide with us,
　Our Lord Emmanuel.

WE THREE KINGS

We three kings of Orient are;
Bearing gifts we traverse afar
Field and fountain, moor and mountain,
Following yonder star:

> *O star of wonder, star of night,*
> *Star with royal beauty bright,*
> *Westward leading, still proceeding,*
> *Guide us to thy perfect light.*

Melchior.
Born a king on Bethlehem plain,
Gold I bring, to crown him again –
King for ever, ceasing never,
Over us all to reign:

Gaspar.
Frankincense to offer have I;
Incense owns a Deity nigh:
Prayer and praising, all men raising,
Worship him, God most high:

Balthazar.
Myrrh is mine; its bitter perfume
Breathes a life of gathering gloom;
Sorrowing, sighing, bleeding, dying,
Sealed in the stone-cold tomb:

All.
Glorious now, behold him arise,
King, and God, and sacrifice!
Heaven sings alleluya,
Alleluya the earth replies:

O star of wonder, star of night,
Star with royal beauty bright,
Westward leading, still proceeding,
Guide us to thy perfect light.

JOHN HENRY HOPKINS

IT CAME UPON THE
MIDNIGHT CLEAR

It came upon the midnight clear,
That glorious song of old,
From angels bending near the earth
To touch their harps of gold:
"Peace on the earth, good will to men,
From heaven's all gracious King."
The world in solemn stillness lay
To hear the angels sing.

Still through the cloven skies they come
With peaceful wings unfurled,
And still their heavenly music floats
O'er all the weary world;
Above its sad and lowly plains
They bend on hovering wing,
And ever o'er its Babel-sounds
The blessed angels sing.

Yet with the woes of sin and strife
The world has suffered long;
Beneath the heavenly hymn have rolled
Two thousand years of wrong;
And warring humankind hears not
The tidings which they bring.

O hush the noise and cease your strife
And hear the angels sing.

For lo! The days are hastening on,
By prophets seen of old,
When with the ever-circling years
Shall come the time foretold,
When peace shall over all the earth
Its ancient splendors fling,
And all the world give back the song
Which now the angels sing.

SILENT NIGHT

Silent night, holy night,
All is calm, all is bright
Round yon virgin mother and child.
Holy infant, so tender and mild,
Sleep in heavenly peace.
Sleep in heavenly peace.

Silent night, holy night,
Shepherds quake at the sight,
Glories stream from heaven afar,
Heavenly hosts sing alleluia;
Christ, the Savior, is born!
Christ, the Savior, is born!

Silent night, holy night,
Son of God, love's pure light
Radiant beams from thy holy face,
With the dawn of redeeming grace,
Jesus, Lord, at thy birth.
Jesus, Lord, at thy birth.

JOSEPH MOHR
    TRANSLATED BY JOHN FREEMAN YOUNG

LO, HOW A ROSE
E'ER BLOOMING

Lo, how a Rose e'er blooming
From tender stem hath sprung!
Of Jesse's lineage coming
As seers of old have sung.
It came, a blossom bright,
Amid the cold of winter,
When half spent was the night.

Isaiah 'twas foretold it,
The Rose I have in mind,
With Mary we behold it,
The Virgin Mother kind.
To show God's love aright,
She bore to us a Savior,
When half spent was the night.

O Flower, whose fragrance tender
With sweetness fills the air,
Dispel in glorious splendor
The darkness everywhere;
True man, yet very God,
From sin and death now save us,
And share our every load.

ANON.   195

THE CHERRY-TREE CAROL

Joseph was an old man,
   and an old man was he,
When he wedded Mary,
   in the land of Galilee.

Joseph and Mary walked
   through an orchard good,
Where was cherries and berries,
   so red as any blood.

Joseph and Mary walked
   through an orchard green,
Where was berries and cherries,
   as thick as might be seen.

O then bespoke Mary,
   so meek and so mild:
"Pluck me one cherry, Joseph,
   for I am with child."

O then bespoke Joseph,
   with words most unkind:
"Let him pluck thee a cherry
   that brought thee with child."

O then bespoke the babe,
    within his mother's womb:
"Bow down then the tallest tree,
    for my mother to have some."

Then bowed down the highest tree
    unto his mother's hand;
Then she cried, "See, Joseph,
    I have cherries at command."

"O eat your cherries, Mary,
    O eat your cherries, now;
O eat your cherries, Mary,
    that grow upon the bough."

As Joseph was a walking,
    he heard an angel sing:
"This night shall be born
    our heavenly king.

"He neither shall be born
    in housen nor in hall,
Nor in the place of Paradise,
    but in an ox's stall.

"He neither shall be clothed
    in purple nor in pall,

But all in fair linen,
    as were babies all.

"He neither shall be rocked
    in silver nor in gold,
But in a wooden cradle,
    that rocks on the mould.

"He neither shall be christened
    in white wine nor red,
But with fair spring water,
    with which we were christened."

Then Mary took her babe,
    and sat him on her knee,
Saying, "My dear son, tell me
    what this world will be."

"O I shall be as dead, mother,
    as the stones in the wall;
O the stones in the streets, mother,
    shall mourn for me all.

"Upon Easter-day, mother,
    my uprising shall be;
O the sun and the moon, mother,
    shall both rise with me."

198   ANON.

I SAW THREE SHIPS

I saw three ships come sailing in,
On Christmas Day, on Christmas Day,
I saw three ships come sailing in,
On Christmas Day in the morning.

And what was in those ships all three?
On Christmas Day, on Christmas Day,
And what was in those ships all three?
On Christmas Day in the morning.

Our Saviour Christ and his lady.
On Christmas Day, on Christmas Day,
Our Saviour Christ and his lady.
On Christmas Day in the morning.

Pray, whither sailed those ships all three?
On Christmas Day, on Christmas Day,
Pray, whither sailed those ships all three?
On Christmas Day in the morning.

O, they sailed into Bethlehem.
On Christmas Day, on Christmas Day,
O, they sailed into Bethlehem.
On Christmas Day in the morning.

And all the bells on earth shall ring,
  On Christmas Day, on Christmas Day,
And all the bells on earth shall ring,
  On Christmas Day in the morning.

And all the angels in Heaven shall sing,
  On Christmas Day, on Christmas Day,
And all the angels in Heaven shall sing,
  On Christmas Day in the morning.

And all the souls on earth shall sing.
  On Christmas Day, on Christmas Day,
And all the souls on earth shall sing.
  On Christmas Day in the morning.

Then let us all rejoice amain!
  On Christmas Day, on Christmas Day,
Then let us all rejoice amain!
  On Christmas Day in the morning.

I SING OF A MAIDEN

I sing of a maiden
   That is makèless;
King of all kings
   To her son she ches.

He came all so still
   Where his mother was,
As dew in April
   That falleth on the grass.

He came all so still
   To his mother's bowr,
As dew in April
   That falleth on the flower.

He came all so still
   Where his mother lay,
As dew in April
   That falleth on the spray.

Mother and maiden
   Was never none but she;
Well may such a lady
   Godès mother be.

ANON.

A CHILD THIS DAY IS BORN

A child this day is born,
   A child of high renown,
Most worthy of a sceptre,
   A sceptre and a crown:

> *Nowell, Nowell, Nowell,*
>   *Nowell, sing all we may,*
> *Because the King of all kings*
>   *Was born this blessed day.*

These tidings shepherds heard,
   In field watching their fold,
Were by an angel unto them
   That night revealed and told:

To whom the angel spoke,
   Saying, "Be not afraid;
Be glad, poor silly shepherds –
   Why are you so dismayed?

"For lo! I bring you tidings
   Of gladness and of mirth,
Which cometh to all people by
   This holy infant's birth":

Then was there with the angel
    An host incontinent
Of heavenly bright soldiers,
    Which from the Highest was sent:

Lauding the Lord our God,
    And his celestial King;
All glory be in Paradise,
    This heavenly host did sing:

And as the angel told them,
    So to them did appear;
They found the young child, Jesus
      Christ,
    With Mary, his mother dear:

    Nowell, Nowell, Nowell,
      Nowell, sing all we may,
    Because the King of all kings
      Was born this blessed day.

ANON.

TO-MORROW SHALL BE MY DANCING DAY

To-morrow shall be my dancing day:
   I would my true love did so chance
To see the legend of my play,
   To call my true love to my dance:

     Sing O my love, O my love, my love, my love;
     This have I done for my true love.

Then was I born of a virgin pure,
   Of her I took fleshly substance;
Thus was I knit to man's nature,
   To call my true love to my dance:

In a manger laid and wrapped I was,
   So very poor, this was my chance,
Betwixt an ox and a silly poor ass,
   To call my true love to my dance:

Then afterwards baptized I was;
   The Holy Ghost on me did glance,
My Father's voice heard from above,
   To call my true love to my dance:

     Sing O my love, O my love, my love, my love;
     This have I done for my true love.

NOWELL SING WE

Nowell sing we, both all and some,
Now Rex pacificus is ycome.
Exortum est in love and lysse.
Now Christ his gree he gan us gysse,
And with his body us brought to bliss,
 Both all and some.

De fructu ventris of Mary bright,
Both God and man in her alight,
Out of disease he did us dight:

Puer natus to us was sent,
To bliss us bought, fro bale us blent,
And else to woe we had ywent:

Lux fulgebit with love and light,
In Mary mild his pennon pight,
In her took kind with manly might:

Gloria tibi, ay, and bliss,
God unto his grace he us wysse,
The rent of heaven that we not miss:

Nowell sing we, both all and some,
Now Rex pacificus is ycome.

ANON.   205

THE FIRST NOWELL

The first Nowell the angel did say
Was to certain poor shepherds in fields as they lay;
In fields where they lay, keeping their sheep,
In a cold winter's night that was so deep:
Nowell, Nowell, Nowell, Nowell,
Born is the King of Israel!

They lookèd up and saw a star,
Shining in the east, beyond them far;
And to the earth it gave great light,
And so it continued both day and night:

And by the light of that same star,
Three Wise Men came from country far;
To seek for a king was their intent,
And to follow the star wheresoever it went:

This star drew nigh to the north-west;
O'er Bethlehem it took its rest,
And there it did both stop and stay
Right over the place where Jesus lay:

Then did they know assuredly
Within that house the King did lie:
One entered in then for to see,
And found the babe in poverty:

Then entered in those Wise Men three,
Fell reverently upon their knee,
And offered there in his presénce
Both gold and myrrh and frankincense:

Between an ox-stall and an ass
This child truly there born he was;
For want of clothing they did him lay
All in the manger, among the hay:

Then let us all with one accord
Sing praises to our heavenly Lord,
That hath made heaven and earth of naught,
And with his blood mankind hath bought:

If we in our time shall do well,
We shall be free from death and hell;
For God hath preparèd for us all
A resting place in general:
Nowell, Nowell, Nowell, Nowell,
Born is the King of Israel!

ANON.

THE HOLLY AND THE IVY

The holly and the ivy,
When they are both full grown,
Of all the trees that are in the wood,
The holly bears the crown:

> *The rising of the sun*
> *And the running of the deer,*
> *The playing of the merry organ,*
> *Sweet singing in the choir.*

The holly bears a blossom,
As white as the lily flower,
And Mary bore sweet Jesus Christ,
To be our sweet Saviour:

The holly bears a berry,
As red as any blood,
And Mary bore sweet Jesus Christ
To do poor sinners good:

The holly bears a prickle,
As sharp as any thorn,
And Mary bore sweet Jesus Christ
On Christmas day in the morn:

The holly bears a bark,
As bitter as any gall,
And Mary bore sweet Jesus Christ
For to redeem us all:

The holly and the ivy,
When they are both full grown,
Of all the trees that are in the wood,
The holly bears the crown:

The rising of the sun
And the running of the deer,
The playing of the merry organ,
Sweet singing in the choir.

ANON.

GREEN GROW'TH THE HOLLY

Green grow'th the holly,
So doth the ivy;
   Though winter blasts blow ne'er so high,
Green grow'th the holly.

Gay are the flowers,
Hedgerows and ploughlands;
   The days grow longer in the sun,
Soft fall the showers.

Full gold the harvest,
Grain for thy labour;
   With God must work for daily bread,
Else, man, thou starvest.

Fast fall the shed leaves,
Russet and yellow;
   But resting-buds are snug and safe
Where swung the dead leaves.

Green grow'th the holly,
So doth the ivy;
   The God of life can never die,
Hope! saith the holly.

THE TWELVE DAYS OF CHRISTMAS

The twelfth day of Christmas,
My true love gave me
Twelve lords a leaping,
Eleven ladies dancing,
Ten pipers piping,
Nine drummers drumming,
Eight maids a milking,
Seven swans a swimming,
Six geese a laying,
Five gold rings,
Four colly birds,
Three French hens,
Two turtle doves, and
A partridge in a pear-tree.

ANON.

GOD REST YOU MERRY GENTLEMEN

God rest you merry gentlemen,
    Let nothing you dismay,
Remember Christ our Saviour
    Was born on Christmas Day,
To save poor souls from Satan's power
    Which had long time gone astray,
And it's tidings of comfort and joy.

From God that is our Father,
    The blessèd Angels came,
Unto some certain Shepherds,
    With tidings of the same;
That there was born in Bethlehem,
    The Son of God by name.
And it's tidings of comfort and joy.

Go, fear not, said God's Angels,
    Let nothing you affright,
For there is born in Bethlehem,
    Of a pure Virgin bright,
One able to advance you,
    And threw down Satan quite.
And it's tidings of comfort and joy.

The Shepherds at those tidings,
    Rejoiced much in mind,
And left their flocks a feeding
    In tempest storms of wind,
And strait they came to Bethlehem,
    The son of God to find.
And it's tidings of comfort and joy.

Now when they came to Bethlehem,
    Where our sweet Saviour lay,
They found him in a manger,
    Where Oxen feed on hay,
The blessed Virgin kneeling down,
    Unto the Lord did pray.
And it's tidings of comfort and joy.

With sudden joy and gladness,
    The Shepherds were beguil'd,
To see the Babe of Israel,
    Before his mother mild,
On them with joy and chearfulness,
    Rejoice each Mother's Child.
And it's tidings of comfort and joy.

Now to the Lord sing praises,
    All you within this place,
Like we true loving Brethren,
    Each other to embrace,
For the merry time of Christmas,
    Is drawing on a pace.
And it's tidings of comfort and joy.

God bless the ruler of this House,
    And send him long to reign,
And many a merry Christmas
    May live to see again.
Among your friends and kindred,
    That live both far and near
And God send you a happy New Year.

WASSAIL, WASSAIL

Wassail, Wassail, all over the town!
Our toast it is white, and our ale it is brown,
Our bowl it is made of the white maple tree;
With the wassailing bowl we'll drink to thee.

So here is to Cherry and to his right cheek,
Pray God send our master a good piece of beef,
And a good piece of beef that may we all see;
With the wassailing bowl we'll drink to thee.

And here is to Dobbin and to his right eye,
Pray God send our master a good Christmas pie,
And a good Christmas pie that may we all see;
With our wassailing bowl we'll drink to thee.

So here is to Broad May and to her broad horn,
May God send our master a good crop of corn,
And a good crop of corn that may we all see;
With the wassailing bowl we'll drink to thee.

And here is to Fillpail and to her left ear,
Pray God send our master a happy New Year,
And a happy New Year as e'er he did see;
With our wassailing bowl we'll drink to thee.

And here is to Colly and to her long tail,
Pray God send our master he never may fail
A bowl of strong beer; I pray you draw near,
And our jolly wassail it's then you shall hear.

Come, butler, come fill us a bowl of the best,
Then we hope that your soul in heaven may rest;
But if you do draw us a bowl of the small,
Then down shall go butler, bowl and all.

Then here's to the maid in the lily white smock,
Who tripped to the door and slipped back the lock!
Who tripped to the door and pulled back the pin,
For to let these jolly wassailers in.

HERE WE COME A-WASSAILING

Here we come a-wassailing
   Among the leaves so green,
Here we come a-wandering,
   So fair to be seen:

     Love and joy come to you,
     And to you your wassail too,
     And God bless you, and send you
     A happy new year.

Our wassail cup is made
   Of the rosemary tree,
And so is your beer
   Of the best barley:

We are not daily beggars
   That beg from door to door,
But we are neighbours' children
   Whom you have seen before:

Call up the butler of this house,
   Put on his golden ring;
Let him bring us up a glass of beer,
   And better we shall sing:

We have got a little purse
    Of stretching leather skin;
We want a little of your money
    To line it well within:

Bring us out a table,
    And spread it with a cloth;
Bring us out a mouldy cheese,
    And some of your Christmas loaf:

God bless the master of this house,
    Likewise the mistress too;
And all the little children
    That round the table go:

Good Master and good Mistress,
    While you're sitting by the fire,
Pray think of us poor children
    Who are wandering in the mire:

Love and joy come to you,
And to you your wassail too,
And God bless you, and send you
A happy new year.

218   ANON.

AFTER CHRISTMAS

From FOR THE TIME BEING

Well, so that is that. Now we must dismantle the tree,
Putting the decorations back into their cardboard
        boxes –
Some have got broken – and carrying them up to
        the attic.
The holly and the mistletoe must be taken down
        and burnt,
And the children got ready for school. There are
        enough
Left-overs to do, warmed-up, for the rest of the week –
Not that we have much appetite, having drunk such
        a lot,
Stayed up so late, attempted – quite unsuccessfully –
To love all of our relatives, and in general
Grossly overestimated our powers. Once again
As in previous years we have seen the actual Vision
        and failed
To do more than entertain it as an agreeable
Possibility, once again we have sent Him away,
Begging though to remain His disobedient servant,
The promising child who cannot keep His word
        for long.
The Christmas Feast is already a fading memory,
And already the mind begins to be vaguely aware
Of an unpleasant whiff of apprehension at the thought

Of Lent and Good Friday which cannot, after all, now
Be very far off. But, for the time being, here we all are,
Back in the moderate Aristotelian city
Of darning and the Eight-Fifteen, where Euclid's
        geometry
And Newton's mechanics would account for our
        experience,
And the kitchen table exists because I scrub it.
It seems to have shrunk during the holidays.
        The streets
Are much narrower than we remembered; we had
        forgotten
The office was as depressing as this. To those who
        have seen
The Child, however dimly, however incredulously,
The Time Being is, in a sense, the most trying time
        of all.
For the innocent children who whispered so excitedly
Outside the locked door where they knew the presents
        to be
Grew up when it opened. Now, recollecting that moment
We can repress the joy, but the guilt remains conscious;
Remembering the stable where for once in our lives
Everything became a You and nothing was an It.
And craving the sensation but ignoring the cause,
We look round for something, no matter what,
        to inhibit

Our self-reflection, and the obvious thing for that
     purpose
Would be some great suffering. So, once we have met
     the Son,
We are tempted ever after to pray to the Father:
"Lead us into temptation and evil for our sake".
They will come, all right, don't worry; probably in
     a form
That we do not expect, and certainly with a force
More dreadful than we can imagine. In the meantime
There are bills to be paid, machines to keep in repair,
Irregular verbs to learn, the Time Being to redeem
From insignificance. The happy morning is over,
The night of agony still to come; the time is noon:
When the Spirit must practise his scales of rejoicing
Without even a hostile audience, and the Soul endure
A silence that is neither for nor against her faith
That God's Will will be done, that, in spite of her
     prayers,
God will cheat no one, not even the world of its triumph.

UNTRIMMING THE TREE

Now all that scintillation is a chore.
What they so recently assembled
Piece by piece in imitation
Of every year for twenty years ago

Each day became more everyday.
The delicate contrivances ignored,
This clutter in a corner of the eye
Now is an hour on the stepladder

And woman's work. This afternoon,
The sunlight brave and January thin
Reflecting on her, she sets down
Lightlier than they lifted them

Angel and orb and cardboard cornucopia,
The candy cane old as the eldest child.
Once she has packed away the annual farm
(Each cotton sheep plump as a thumb),

Hanging the glassy surface of the lake
Up on its hook in the back bedroom,
She sends the snowy field out to the laundry.
Arms full of a great weightlessness she arises

Toward the airless year in the black attic.
The Season's Greetings flutter in the trash
Out in the alley and the tree,
Naked, imitates mere nature.

All's done but this – that at the last she blind
The windows of the Advent Calendar
From which next year again shall stare
The forest animals as day by day,

As the great Day approaches
Until the Manger stands revealed,
Husband and child and wife, restored
Out of the storm, once more shall be assembled.

JOHN N. MORRIS

BURNING THE CHRISTMAS GREENS

Their time past, pulled down
cracked and flung to the fire
– go up in a roar

All recognition lost, burnt clean
clean in the flame, the green
dispersed, a living red,
flame red, red as blood wakes
on the ash –

and ebbs to a steady burning
the rekindled bed become
a landscape of flame

At the winter's midnight
we went to the trees, the coarse
holly, the balsam and
the hemlock for their green

At the thick of the dark
the moment of the cold's
deepest plunge we brought branches
cut from the green trees

to fill our need, and over
doorways, about paper Christmas
bells covered with tinfoil
and fastened by red ribbons

we stuck the green prongs
in the windows hung
woven wreaths and above pictures
the living green. On the

mantle we built a green forest
and among those hemlock
sprays put a herd of small
white deer as if they

were walking there. All this!
and it seemed gentle and good
to us. Their time past,
relief! The room bare. We

stuffed the dead grate
with them upon the half burnt out
log's smoldering eye, opening
red and closing under them

and we stood there looking down.
Green is a solace
a promise of peace, a fort
against the cold (though we

did not say so) a challenge
above the snow's
hard shell. Green (we might
have said) that, where

small birds hide and dodge
and lift their plaintive
rallying cries, blocks for them
and knocks down

the unseeing bullets of
the storm. Green spruce boughs
pulled down by a weight of
snow – Transformed!

Violence leaped and appeared.
Recreant! roared to life
as the flame rose through and
our eyes recoiled from it.

In the jagged flames green
to red, instant and alive. Green!
those sure abutments ... Gone!
lost to mind

and quick in the contracting
tunnel of the grate
appeared a world! Black
mountains, black and red – as

yet uncolored – and ash white,
an infant landscape of shimmering
ash and flame and we, in
that instant, lost,

breathless to be witnesses,
as if we stood
ourselves refreshed among
the shining fauna of that fire.

NEW YEAR'S EVE

Midnight the years last day the last
high hour the verge where the dancers comet
(loved water lapsing under the bridge
and blood dear blood by the bridged aorta
where the dreaming soul leans distant-eyed
long-watching the flood and its spoil borne seaward)

and I one fleck on the numbered face
one dot on the star-aswarming heaven
stand here in this street of all our streets
of all our times this moment only
the bells the snow the neon   faces
each our own but estranged and fleeing

from a bar all tinkle and red fluorescence
a boy in a tux with tie uneven
puppy-clumsy with auldlangsyning
plaintive so droll came crying Sally
Salleee again and Saalleee louder
a violin teased   he passed in laughter

yet under the heart of each up vein
up brain and loud in the lonely spirit
a-rang desire for Sallys name
or another name or a street or season

not to be conjured by any horn
nor flavored gin nor the flung confetti

o watcher upover the world look down
through gale of stars to the globes blue hover
and see arising in troubled mist
from firefly towns and the dark between them
the waif appeal from lackland hearts
to Sallys name or perhaps anothers

NEW YEAR

Word of endless adoration,
    Christ, I to thy call appear;
On my knees in meek prostration
    To begin a better year.

Spirits in eternal waiting,
    Special ministers of pray'r,
Which our welcome antedating,
    Shall the benediction bear.

Which, the type of vows completed,
    Shall the wreathed garland send,
While new blessings are intreated,
    And communicants attend.

Emblem of the hopes beginning,
    Who the budding rods shall bind,
Way from guiltless nature's winning,
    In good-will to human kind.

Ye that dwell with cherub-turtles
    Mated in that upmost light,
Or parade amongst the myrtles,
    On your steeds of speckl'd white.

Ye that sally from the portal
    Of yon everlasting bow'rs,
Sounding symphonies immortal,
    Years, and months, and days, and hours.

But nor myrtles, nor the breathing
    Of the never-dying grove,
Nor the chaplets sweetly wreathing,
    And by hands angelic wove;

Not the Musick or the mazes
    Of those spirits aptly tim'd,
Can avail like pray'r and praises
    By the Lamb himself sublim'd.

Take ye therefore what ye give him,
    Of his fulness grace for grace,
Strive to think him, speak him, live him,
    Till you find him face to face.

Sing like David, or like Hannah,
    As the spirit first began,
To the God of heights hosanna!
    Peace and charity to man.

Christ his blessing universal
　　On th'arch-patriarch's seed bestow,
Which attend to my rehearsal
　　Of melodious pray'r below.

NEW YEAR'S DAY

Again and then again ... the year is born
To ice and death, and it will never do
To skulk behind storm-windows by the stove
To hear the postgirl sounding her French horn
When the thin tidal ice is wearing through.
Here is the understanding not to love
Each other, or tomorrow that will sieve
Our resolutions. While we live, we live

To snuff the smoke of victims. In the snow
The kitten heaved its hindlegs, as if fouled,
And died. We bent it in a Christmas box
And scattered blazing weeds to scare the crow
Until the snake-tailed sea-winds coughed and howled
For alms outside the church whose double locks
Wait for St. Peter, the distorted key.
Under St. Peter's bell the parish sea

Swells with its smelt into the burlap shack
Where Joseph plucks his hand-lines like a harp,
And hears the fearful *Puer natus est*
Of Circumcision, and relives the wrack
And howls of Jesus whom he holds. How sharp
The burden of the Law before the beast:
Time and the grindstone and the knife of God.
The Child is born in blood, O child of blood.

NEW YEAR POEM

The short afternoon ends, and the year is over;
Above trees at the end of the garden the sky is
        unchanged,
An endless sky; and the wet streets, as ever,
Between standing houses are empty and unchallenged.
From roads where men go home I walk apart
– The buses bearing their loads away from works,
Through the dusk the bicycles coming home from
        bricks –
There evening like a derelict lorry is alone and mute.

These houses are deserted, felt over smashed windows,
No milk on the step, a note pinned to the door
Telling of departure: only shadows
Move when in the day the sun is seen for an hour,
Yet to me this decaying landscape has its uses:
To make me remember, who am always inclined to
        forget,
That there is always a changing at the root,
And a real world in which time really passes.

For even together, outside this shattered city
And its obvious message, if we had lived in that peace
Where the enormous years pass over lightly
– Yes, even there, if I looked into your face

Expecting a word or a laugh on the old conditions,
It would not be a friend who met my eye,
Only a stranger would smile and turn away,
Not one of the two who first performed these actions.

For sometimes it is shown to me in dreams
The Eden that all wish to recreate
Out of their living, from their favourite times;
The miraculous play where all their dead take part,
Once more articulate; or the distant ones
They will never forget because of an autumn talk
By a railway, an occasional glimpse in a public park,
Any memory for the most part depending on chance.

And seeing this through that I know that to be wrong,
Knowing by the flower the root that seemed so
      harmless
Dangerous; and all must take their warning
From these brief dreams of unsuccessful charms,
Their aloof visions of delight, where Desire
And Fear work hand-in-glove like medicals
To produce the same results. The bells
That we used to await will not be rung this year,

So it is better to sleep and leave the bottle unopened;
Tomorrow in the offices the year on the stamps will
      be altered;

Tomorrow new diaries consulted, new calendars stand;
With such small adjustments life will again move
  forward
Implicating us all; and the voice of the living be heard:
"It is to us that you should turn your straying
  attention;
Us who need you, and are affected by your fortune;
Us you should love and to whom you should give
  your word."

TWELFTH NIGHT

Down from the window take the withered holly.
Feed the torn tissue to the literal blaze.
Now, now at last are come the melancholy
Anticlimatic days.

Here in the light of morning, hard, unvarnished,
Let us with haste dismantle the tired tree
Of ornaments, a trifle chipped and tarnished,
Pretend we do not see

How all the rooms seem shabbier and meaner
And the tired house a little less than snug.
Fold up the tinsel. Run the vacuum cleaner
Over the littered rug.

Nothing is left. The postman passes by, now,
Bearing no gifts, no kind or seasonal word.
The icebox yields no wing, no nibbled thigh, now,
From any holiday bird.

Sharp in the streets the north wind plagues its betters
While Christmas snow to gutters is consigned.
Nothing remains except the thank-you letters,
Most tedious to the mind,

And the gilt gadget (duplicated) which is
Marked for exchange at Abercrombie-Fitch's.

TWELFTH NIGHT

It has always been King Herod that I feared;
   King Herod and his kinsmen, ever since . . .
I do not like the colour of your beard;
   I think that you are wicked, and a prince.

I keep no stable . . . how your horses stamp! . . .
   If you are wise men, you will leave me soon;
I have been frightened by a thievish tramp
   Who counted bloody silver in the moon.

You get no lodging underneath these roofs,
   No, though you pay in frankincense and myrrh;
Your harness jangles with your horses' hooves;
   Be quiet; you will wake him if you stir.

This is no church for Zoroastrians,
   Nor resting-place for governors from Rome;
Oh, I have knowledge of your secret plans;
   Your faces are familiar; go home.

And you, young captain of the lion stare,
   Subdue your arrogance to this advice;
You should forbid your soldiery to swear,
   To spit at felons, and to play at dice.

You have perceived, above the chimney ledge,
    Hanging inverted by Saint David's harp,
His sword from heaven, with the double edge
    Which, for your service, is no longer sharp.

He sleeps, like some ingenuous shepherd boy
    Or carpenter's apprentice, but his slim
And wounded hands shall never more destroy
    Another giant; do not waken him.

The counterpane conceals the deeper wound
    Which lately I have washed with vinegar;
Now let this iron bar be importuned;
    I say you shall not speak to him of war.

EPIPHANY

Unearthly lightning of presage
In any dark day's iron age
May come to lift the hair and bless
Even our tired earthliness,

And sundown bring an age of gold,
Forgèd in faëry, far and old,
An elsewhere and an elfin light,
And kings rise eastward in the night.

ACKNOWLEDGMENTS

Thanks are due to the following copyright holders for their permission to reprint translations in this anthology:

ACHEBE, CHINUA: 'Christmas in Biafra (1969)' from *Christmas in Biafra and Other Poems* by Chinua Achebe. Copyright © 1973 by Chinua Achebe. Used by permission of Doubleday, a division of Random House, Inc. AUDEN, W. H.: from 'For the Time Being' from *The Collected Poems.* Reprinted by permission of Vintage Books, a division of Random House, Inc. BETJEMAN, JOHN: 'Christmas' from *A Few Late Chrysanthemums* (1954). Reprinted by permission of Transatlantic Arts, Inc. BISHOP, MORRIS: 'The Dark Christmas on Wildwood Road' from *A Bowl of Bishop* by Morris Bishop. Copyright 1954 by Morris Bishop. Used by permission of Doubleday, a division of Random House, Inc. CHESTERTON, G. K.: 'Joseph' from *Chapters into Verse Vol II*, published by Oxford University Press. Reprinted by permission of A. P. Watt Ltd. on behalf of The Royal Literary Fund. DAVIS, DICK: 'A Christmas Poem' from *A Kind of Love*, University of Arkansas Press, 1991, rights reverted. Reprinted by permission of the author. DAY-LEWIS, C.: 'The Christmas Tree' and 'A Carol' from *The Complete Poems* by C. Day-Lewis, published by Sinclair-Stevenson (1992). Copyright in this edition the Estate of C. Day-Lewis. DE LA MARE, WALTER: 'Christmas Eve' from *The Complete Poems of Walter de la Mare* (USA, 1970) reprinted with permission from The Literary Trustees of Walter de la Mare, and the Society of Authors as their representative. DICKINSON, EMILY: 'The Savior must have been a docile Gentleman' from *The Complete Poems of Emily Dickinson.* Thomas H. Johnson, ed., Cambridge, Mass: The Belknap Press of Harvard University Press, Copyright © 1951, 1955, 1976, 1983 by the President and Fellows of Harvard College. Reprinted by permission of the publishers and the Trustees of Amherst College. ELIOT, T. S.: 'The Journey of the Magi' from *Collected Poems 1909–1962* by T. S. Eliot, copyright 1936 by Harcourt, Inc., copyright © 1964, 1963 by T. S. Eliot, reprinted by permission of the

245

publisher. FIELD, EUGENE: 'Jest 'fore Christmas' from *The Poems of Eugene Field*, published by Charles Scribner's Sons, New York, 1910. Reprinted by permission of Simon & Schuster. GRAVES, ROBERT: 'Christmas Robin' from *Collected Poems*, published by Carcanet Press. Reprinted by permission of A. P. Watt Ltd. HEATH-STUBBS, JOHN: 'For the Nativity' from *Collected Poems 1943–1987*, published by Carcanet Press. Reprinted by permission of David Higham Associates. HECHT, ANTHONY: 'Illumination' and 'Christmas is Coming' from *Collected Earlier Poems* by Anthony Hecht. Copyright © 1990 by Anthony E. Hecht. Reprinted by permission of Alfred A. Knopf, Inc. HUGHES, LANGSTON: 'Shepherd's Song at Christmas' from *Collected Poems* by Langston Hughes. Copyright © 1994 by the Estate of Langston Hughes. Reprinted by permission of Alfred A. Knopf, Inc. JENNINGS, ELIZABETH: 'The Annunciation' from *Collected Poems* by Elizabeth Jennings, published by Carcanet Press. Reprinted by permission of David Higham Associates. KIPLING, RUDYARD: 'A Nativity 1914–18' and 'Christmas in India' from *Rudyard Kipling's Verse, Inclusive Edition*, 1931. Reprinted with permission from A. P. Watt Ltd. On behalf of The National Trust for Places of Historic Interest or Natural Beauty. LARKIN, PHILIP: 'New Year Poem' from *Collected Poems* by Philip Larkin. Copyright © 1988, 1989 by the Estate of Philip Larkin. Reprinted by permission of Farrar, Straus and Giroux, LLC. LEWIS, JANET: 'A Lullaby' from *Poems 1924–1944* by Janet Lewis, published by Swallow Press, 1950. Reprinted with the permission of Ohio University Press/Swallow Press, Athens, Ohio. LOWELL, ROBERT: 'New Year's Day' from *Lord Weary's Castle*. Copyright 1947 by Harcourt, Inc. Reprinted by permission of the publisher. MCCLATCHY, J. D.: 'An Old Song Ended' from *The Rest of the Way* by J. D. McClatchy. Copyright © 1990 by J. D. McClatchy. Reprinted by permission of Alfred A. Knopf, Inc. MCGINLEY, PHYLLIS: 'City Christmas', copyright 1935 by Phyllis McGinley, 'Office Party', copyright 1932–1960 by Phyllis McGinley; Copyright 1938–42, 1944, 1945, 1958, 1959 by the Curtis Publishing Co., 'Lady Selecting her Christmas Cards', 'Twelfth Night', copyright 1940 by Phyllis McGinley, renewed, from *Times Three* by Phyllis McGinley. Used by permission of Viking Penguin, a division of Penguin Putnam Inc.

247

INDEX OF AUTHORS

250

254